Black Americans of Achievement
LEGACY EDITION

Oprah Winfrey

TALK SHOW HOST AND MEDIA MAGNATE

Sherry Beck Paprocki

Checkmark Books®
An imprint of Infobase Publishing

Oprah Winfrey

Copyright © 2006, 2008 by Infobase Publishing

Checkmark Books
An imprint of Infobase Publishing
132 West 31st Street
New York NY 10001

ISBN-13: 978-0-7910-9226-2 (hardcover)
ISBN-13: 978-1-60413-326-4 (pbk.)

Library of Congress Cataloging-in-Publication Data
Paprocki, Sherry.
  Oprah Winfrey / Sherry Paprocki.
     p. cm. — (Black Americans of achievement, legacy edition)
  Includes bibliographical references and index.
  ISBN 0-7910-9226-7 (hardcover)
  1. Winfrey, Oprah. 2. Television personalities—United States—Biography. 3. African American television personalities—Biography. 4. Actors—United States—Biography. 5. African American actors—United States—Biography. I. Title. II. Series.
  PN1992.4.W56P35 2006
  791.4502'8'092—dc22   2006004577

Series design by Keith Trego
Cover design by Keith Trego and Takeshi Takahashi

Printed in the United States of America

Bang Hermitage 10 9 8 7 6 5 4 3 2 1

This book is printed on acid-free paper.

Contents

Christmas in South Africa

Sun streamed through the window as Oprah Winfrey entered the hospital room. She was there with nine-year-old Esona, whose mother was dying of AIDS in this South African hospital. Esona was glad to have Winfrey along for the visit, and her mother smiled at them as they entered the room. Although Esona's mother was thin and frail as she lay in the hospital bed, her eyes were wide while she chatted with her visitors.

Winfrey met Esona at one of the parties held at schools and orphanages during the talk show host's ChristmasKindness tour in 2002. On the tour, Winfrey was accompanied by plenty of helpers and truckloads of gifts, including dolls, soccer balls, clothing, and food. More than one million South African children, such as Esona, had lost or would lose their parents to the AIDS epidemic, and many more people were expected to die. Winfrey wanted the orphans of the country to know that someone cared about them.

It was painful to see Esona's mom so sick, lying in a hospital bed, just a few months away from death. Winfrey was appalled that day when she was told that the hospital did not have any of the medications needed to treat AIDS. Her face crumpled in tears. "That makes no sense to me," she cried, as her video crew taped the scene.

After talking with Esona's mother, Winfrey held the woman's hand and told her that she had a strong spirit. Esona put a picture from the ChristmasKindness party on the hospital nightstand and stretched to hug her mom in the bed. Together, she and Winfrey left the room. They hugged, quietly, in the hospital hallway.

The hospital visit was one of the video clips that Winfrey posted on her Web site after the ChristmasKindness tour.

Hundreds of children in Durban, South Africa, turned out on December 8, 2002, for a stop on Oprah Winfrey's ChristmasKindness tour. Many of the children were orphans whose parents died of AIDS. Winfrey gave them gifts of food, clothing, school supplies, and toys during her philanthropic trip.

Meeting Esona and many children like her affected Winfrey in very special ways. Winfrey knew that most of the children she would visit had never received a gift in their lives. She took a big white tent with her wherever she went and held at least 12 parties in 12 places. Nearly every day, she and her helpers set up the big tent at a new site and prepared for a party that hundreds of children would attend. The children were there at holiday time with no food, no family, and only the shoes and clothes they were wearing. Still, they laughed and sang, played games and talked. They grinned big, toothy smiles when Winfrey showered them with gifts. When her trip was over, Winfrey was elated that the children had been so grateful. The tour was one of the best experiences of her life. "This Christmas in South Africa, my life was sweetened 50,000 times over," she said. "I've always felt that life is sweeter when you share."

A KINDNESS FROM THE PAST

Oprah Winfrey still remembers a time when she was a child and some adults shared with her. She was 12 years old and living with her mother. There was not enough money to buy Christmas presents. A group of Catholic nuns visited her house and gave her a baby doll. She was very glad to have gotten the gift because it was the only one she received that year. She was also happy that she would have something to say when the other children at school asked her what she got for Christmas.

Winfrey had a sad and lonely life as a child, first living with her poor grandmother, moving once to live with her mother, and moving again to live with her father. Winfrey knows what it is like to be a young girl left on her own. She also knows what it is like to feel lonely and to have no one to talk to. Perhaps that is why she was so saddened when she heard about the plight of so many South African children.

Winfrey apparently learned a great deal during that trip in 2002. Esona told her that students in South Africa were not being taught about AIDS, a fatal disease that had killed more than 17 million people in sub-Saharan Africa, which includes South Africa and other African countries south of the Sahara Desert. Millions more are expected to die in the years to come. At least 12 million children have been orphaned in sub-Saharan Africa because their parents have died of AIDS, and an estimated 2 million children there under the age of 15 have the disease. Many babies will be born with the disease, which is passed on to them from their mothers. The South African government and many of the people who live there are too poor to buy much of the medication that helps people with AIDS and its precursor, HIV.

Winfrey was overwhelmed with sadness for the thousands of South African children who no longer had parents to take care of them. During her trip, she also visited a wood and mud hut where two young girls had lived alone since their mother died of AIDS the year before. Fifteen-year-old Thanda began to cry when Winfrey asked about her mother. Winfrey promised the girl that she would get to go to school and that she and her sister would have dresses and uniforms to wear. Thanda told Winfrey that she wanted to be a doctor.

"I'm going to make sure you get to school," Winfrey said, as she patted the girl on her back. "And if you want to be a doctor, you can be a doctor. We're going to do everything we can to make sure you become a doctor." Winfrey gave the young girl a big hug as she left.

Also during her trip in South Africa, Winfrey visited an orphanage called God's Golden Acre, where 72 children lived without their parents. While she was there, Winfrey met a young girl named Kandysile. The girl kept staring at the ground and wouldn't look up so Winfrey could see her eyes. Winfrey bent over and was nearly upside down trying to look into the girl's face. Finally, Kandysile looked at her.

"You must always hold your head up," Winfrey sternly told her. "You must keep your head held high. Because you're a strong, proud girl."

Winfrey was trying to teach the young girl to have confidence in herself even though she and many of the children in South Africa had extremely difficult lives. They had no parents and very little to eat, and they didn't even know if anyone cared about them. Winfrey wanted the children to know that, even though they were poor, they could still be successful in life. Winfrey attributes her own success partly to the help and encouragement she received from a few important people when she was a teenager.

The Oprah Winfrey Show has been the top talk show since it first appeared on television 20 years ago. During her show, Winfrey speaks frequently about the value of a good education. She acknowledges that her education helped her get her first job in television when she was a college student. She knows that if she had not attended college, she might never have been able to get a full-time job in broadcasting. In fact, without her formal education, Winfrey might have never left behind her life of poverty in Mississippi.

FOUNDING AN ACADEMY

Winfrey honored the young women of South Africa during that trip when she announced the opening of the Oprah Winfrey Leadership Academy for Girls, a 22-acre boarding school in the Gauteng Province. Winfrey convinced the South African Ministry of Education and her friend Nelson Mandela, who is the former president of South Africa, to help build the school. Winfrey's private fund, the Oprah Winfrey Foundation, gave $10 million toward the project. The school was established especially for South African girls who are academically talented and exhibit leadership skills.

"Education is the way to move mountains, to build bridges, to change the world," Winfrey said. "Education is the path to the future. I believe that education is indeed freedom. With God's help, these girls will be the future leaders on the path to peace in South Africa."

Oprah Winfrey and Nelson Mandela, the former president of South Africa, break ground on the Oprah Winfrey Leadership Academy for Girls in Meyerton, South Africa. "Education is the way to move mountains, to build bridges, to change the world," Winfrey said.

IN HER OWN WORDS...

On December 6, 2002, Oprah Winfrey was joined by Nelson Mandela and several others for the groundbreaking of the Oprah Winfrey Leadership Academy for Girls in South Africa. In announcing plans for the academy, Winfrey said:

I believe that one of the world's most important resources is its young people, and I believe education gives young people a greater voice in their own lives and helps them to create a brighter future for themselves and their communities.

Back in Chicago, where *The Oprah Winfrey Show* is produced, Winfrey spent months planning the school. She visited an all-girls school on Chicago's South Side to get ideas for the academy. Winfrey wanted the girls of South Africa to have the best education she could possibly give them. "It is very important to me that the school reflects the spirit of this community," Winfrey said when construction of the academy began. "I will be overseeing even the smallest details.... This is the girls' home. They need a fireplace in the wintertime to read. So, we will have a fireplace in the library." Plans for the school included up-to-date classrooms, computer and science labs, an auditorium/gymnasium, an amphitheater, a sports field, modern dorm facilities, and a dining hall.

After her ChristmasKindness trip to South Africa, Winfrey presented the story of her travels during one of her shows. Viewers were so moved that they donated $7 million to Oprah's Angel Network, a charity organization she had established a few years earlier. Through it, her fans can make donations to worthwhile causes. Winfrey planned to spend the money on medication for mothers who have HIV, counseling for children whose lives are affected by AIDS, books, school supplies, school uniforms for children, and teachers' salaries.

Winfrey accomplished a great deal during her trip to South Africa, and she has visited several more times since. The popular talk show host has used her intellect, her education, and her personal experiences to build a life that many people only dream about. She started a magazine, founded television- and film-production companies, and created a charity that gives away millions of dollars each year. Some people say that Winfrey is the most powerful woman in the world. Through her television show, seen in 121 countries, she is known by people around the world. Despite her enormous fame, wealth, and influence, however, it seems that Winfrey remains a down-to-earth Mississippi girl who is interested in learning about other people and how she can help those in need.

2

Growing Up Poor

Oprah Gail Winfrey was born to a young, poor mother on January 29, 1954, in a farmhouse in Kosciusko, Mississippi. Her name was supposed to be Orpah, from the Book of Ruth in the Bible, but the letters got mixed up on her birth certificate so she was named Oprah instead. Her mother, Vernita Lee, and her father, Vernon Winfrey, were never married.

Vernita was only 18 when Oprah was born, and she was unable to provide the things that her baby needed. Oprah's father was in the army at the time. He didn't even know he had a daughter until a birth announcement arrived with a message asking him to send clothes for the baby. Oprah's grandmother, Hattie Mae Lee, was the first person in Oprah's life to provide her with stability. Until she was six years old, Oprah lived with her grandmother and grandfather—a man who she says seemed very scary at the time—on a farm in rural Mississippi. The home had no electricity, and Oprah had to use an outhouse because there was no indoor bathroom. The house had no indoor plumbing, so one of little Oprah's chores was to haul water indoors from the well, which was several feet from the house.

There were no other children for miles around. Oprah spent her days playing alone most of the time. She had few toys, so for entertainment she sometimes talked to the cows and the pigs on the farm. She took big leaps off the front porch and played with a corncob doll that her grandmother made for her. Oprah's grandmother made her clothes, and they ate whatever they grew on the farm. The family sold eggs to earn extra money. Oprah learned to love many foods that her grandmother cooked; some dishes that she enjoyed would become a problem as she fought a long battle with her weight as an adult. Oprah loved buttermilk cornbread, fried green tomatoes, fried okra, fried chicken, greens cooked with hamhocks, and her grandmother's biscuits. At night, she and her grandmother slept together in a featherbed while her grandfather slept in another room.

In Mississippi, Oprah never wore shoes, unless it was Sunday. Then she put on her shiny black patent leather shoes and wore them to the nearby Baptist church. Her grandmother must have known that Oprah was a smart little girl because she taught her to read before she even started school. Oprah has said that reading was her outlet to the real world. With her grandmother's encouragement, Oprah quickly memorized Bible verses.

Oprah loved to talk and recite the Bible at church as well as in front of people. The women of the church would whisper about Oprah being gifted, and Hattie Mae was very proud. At home, however, her grandmother believed that children should be seen and not heard. So, when company came to the house, Oprah was required to sit quietly and not say a word. Hattie Mae was very strict. When she thought that the little girl had done something wrong, she would insist that Oprah go outside to get a switch. Oprah would shudder. She knew the switch would be used to whip her. Oprah said she got a whipping nearly every day—it didn't matter what she did, if she spilled something, if she told a story. It seemed as if there were many reasons why she was whipped. Sometimes the whippings would be so bad she would get welts on her back.

Yet, Oprah's grandmother was also her biggest supporter. She made Oprah believe that she could accomplish anything that she wanted to in her life.

Oprah was four years old when her mother decided to move to Wisconsin alone to try to build a better life. Oprah stayed on the farm with her grandparents and started school the following year, when she was five, in the nearby town of Buffalo. The little girl who could already read and write realized that she was probably smarter than her classmates. Her teacher agreed, and Oprah was quickly promoted to the first grade. She stayed at the Buffalo school, though, only a short time. When she was six years old, Oprah's mother wanted her to come live with her in Wisconsin. By that time, Vernita had a job as a maid and had given birth to another daughter, who was named Patricia. They rented a room from Patricia's godmother in the busy city of Milwaukee.

As a young girl, Oprah had admired white children. She thought they never got whippings, and she wanted to be like them. She was a fan of Shirley Temple, a young actress with curly blond hair and a cute little nose. A few years later, though, when Oprah was 10, she took note of the beautiful Diana Ross and the Supremes when they appeared on *The Ed Sullivan Show*. It was the first time Oprah had ever seen a black woman who was beautiful and successful. She decided that she wanted to be just like Diana Ross when she grew up. Oprah also marveled at Sidney Poitier as she watched him on television the night he became the first black man to win an Academy Award for best actor.

The Supremes, (from left) Florence Ballard, Diana Ross, and Mary Wilson, performed on *The Ed Sullivan Show* in December 1964. When 10-year-old Oprah Winfrey watched Ross and the Supremes on the program, it was the first time she ever saw beautiful and successful black women on television.

ANOTHER MOVE

Generally, Oprah didn't much like her new home in Milwaukee. It was small and crowded. The city seemed dirty and noisy compared with life on the farm. Instead of having cows and pigs as her pets, Oprah remembered playing with cockroaches. She captured them, put them in jars, and gave them names. Within a few years, Vernita realized that she couldn't take care of her talkative, provocative daughter. Oprah was sent to live with people who were strangers—her father, Vernon Winfrey, and his wife, Zelma.

Vernon Winfrey had been discharged from the army in 1955 and had a job in Nashville, Tennessee, as a janitor at Vanderbilt University. He had a second job, which paid only 75 cents an hour, as a pot washer at Nashville's City Hospital. Vernon owned a small, brick house, and Oprah had a room all to herself. Vernon and Zelma were unable to have children, so Oprah was the center of their lives.

Zelma quickly realized that Oprah was gifted in reading, but Zelma panicked the summer before Oprah was to enter the third grade. She discovered that Oprah knew very little math. That summer, she taught Oprah to memorize the multiplication tables so she would be prepared to enter school in the fall. Oprah was eight years old when she received a box of 64 crayons and a stack of white paper as Christmas gifts from her father and stepmother. Her stepmother wouldn't allow her to take the crayons and paper to school, though, because she knew Oprah would give them all away to other children. Young Oprah Winfrey had a generous soul.

One of the first things Oprah did when she got to Nashville was to get her library card. Oprah was pleased that day because reading was important to her. Her teacher at Wharton Elementary School realized that Oprah was smart, and once again, she was moved ahead to a higher grade. In the meantime, Oprah started reciting Bible verses and sermons at her father's church. She so impressed the local folks that Vernon and Zelma eventually started driving her all over Tennessee to speak in churches. Oprah even preached to other children on the playground, earning the nickname "The Preacher."

BACK TO MILWAUKEE

At the end of the school year, Oprah went back to Milwaukee to visit her mother and half-sister, Patricia. Oprah's mother had given birth to another baby, Oprah's half-brother, Jeffrey. At the end of the summer, Oprah's mother pleaded with Vernon Winfrey, who had driven from Nashville to pick up his child. She wanted Oprah to stay in Milwaukee. Vernon agreed even though he was sad to leave Oprah behind. It didn't take long, though, for Oprah to discover that her mother—who still worked as a maid—had little time for her. Oprah spent much of her free time watching television. Oprah's mother didn't appreciate books the way her father and Zelma did. So, unlike Nashville, Oprah didn't enjoy Milwaukee much. Her half-brother and half-sister took up most of her mother's time. She felt as if her half-sister, who had much lighter skin, was the center of attention. And, unlike in Nashville, no one seemed to notice that Oprah was smart. Instead, she was teased for sitting around reading all the time.

Perhaps the most difficult period of Oprah's life began when she was nine years old. Her mother left her and her half-siblings at the home of a relative, where Oprah was raped by her 19-year-old cousin. Oprah felt violated and ashamed. She thought she had done something wrong. It was years before she told anyone what had happened. Over the next few years, she was raped by others—her mother's boyfriend and an uncle. Oprah became a different person; her life seemed totally changed. And, she felt as if no one in her mother's family would believe what was happening to her. "I blamed myself," Oprah told a *Washington Post* writer in 1986. "I was always very needy, always in need of attention, and they just took advantage of that."

Without any real guidance and no adult in whom she could really place her trust, Oprah grew into a promiscuous young teenager. She sought attention from boys, because she knew she could get attention from them. No longer was Oprah, the preacher, admired for her speaking abilities.

Fortunately, a teacher at Lincoln Middle School in Milwaukee finally recognized Oprah's academic talents, and he knew Oprah could do well in a better environment. The teacher helped her get a scholarship to attend a private high school called Nicolet, which was in one of Milwaukee's wealthiest suburbs. Again, Oprah's life was changing.

A TROUBLED TEENAGER

Oprah was the only black student at Nicolet, and she seemed to be very popular because of that. Her more affluent classmates, who had their own maids and black servants, invited her into their homes. Oprah was envious of some of these students, and her experiences at Nicolet led her to become angrier with her mother and the lifestyle that they led.

Oprah's anger caused her to take some inappropriate actions. She lied about her lifestyle to her classmates, and she lied to her mother. She stole money from her mother's purse. She once was so angry with her mother that she tore apart their apartment, called the police, and then lied about what had happened. She told the police that she had been attacked by a burglar. Oprah had more angry tirades and arguments with her mother. She stayed out late. Finally, she ran away. "I started acting out my need for attention, my need to be loved," Oprah recalled during her interview with the *Washington Post* writer. "My mother didn't have the time."

Oprah's mother tried to have her admitted to a juvenile detention facility, but Oprah was turned away because there were no available beds. Oprah's promiscuity continued. She became pregnant when she was 14 years old. She didn't tell her mother or her father until it was nearly time to give birth.

Reports vary about where Oprah gave birth—she may have gone back to live with her father in Tennessee, or she may have been living with her mother until she delivered. The baby died within days after it was born. After this, Oprah would live in Nashville with her father. Vernon Winfrey did not know about all the sexual abuse his daughter had suffered, but he did know she needed some rules. She was required to be in by 11:00 P.M. She wasn't allowed to wear a lot of make-up, and she had to put away her halter tops and her shortest skirts. Vernon also recognized that Oprah needed some guidance when it came to relationships with boys. "If I hadn't been sent to live with my father, I would have gone in another direction," Oprah said. "I could have made a good criminal."

Vernon Winfrey's life had changed while Oprah was in Milwaukee. He was now a businessman, with his own barbershop in Nashville. He still found time, however, to talk to Oprah and help her get on track. Vernon's years of working on Vanderbilt's campus had left an impression on him. He knew that Oprah was smart enough to attend college, so he and Zelma continued to stress studying and good grades. Throughout the rest of high school and into her career, Oprah never again spent time living with her mother.

A TURNAROUND

Despite her difficult early years, Oprah straightened out her life. She was one of the first black students to attend the newly desegregated East High School in Nashville, and she was a standout student. Her early love of reading continued. Her stepmother exposed her to the works of many important African-American authors. In addition, Oprah enjoyed the *Diary of Anne Frank*, the story of Helen Keller, and the life of Sojourner Truth, an abolitionist and women's rights activist who lived in the nineteenth century. Perhaps because of her life's experiences, Oprah was enthralled by stories of women who had overcome huge obstacles.

But, at first, Oprah was less excited about the extra school-work her father and stepmother required. Getting C's on her report card was not good enough for Oprah's father. And, Oprah's parents required her to write reports about the library books she read for pleasure. There was one book that made an

In high school, Oprah Winfrey enjoyed reading about the life of Sojourner Truth, the nineteenth-century abolitionist, shown here in 1864. Oprah was touched by stories of women who had overcome great obstacles.

especially big impression. In 1970, when she was 16 years old, Oprah read Maya Angelou's book, *I Know Why the Caged Bird Sings*. Around the same time, Oprah resumed speaking at her father's Baptist church and other local churches and clubs. Certainly, Oprah Winfrey was a woman who had a gift for speaking.

IN HER OWN WORDS...

Stories of courageous women made an impression on Oprah Winfrey in her youth. That admiration continues to this day. In 2005, Winfrey held a week-end celebration at her California home to honor 25 women she considers legends in their time. Here is what she wrote in *O, The Oprah Magazine*, about how the Legends Weekend began:

I started thinking about all the women who'd come before me, many of whom have now passed on—women whose steps created a journey of no boundaries for my generation. I wanted to thank them, celebrate them, and rejoice in their spirit.

At East High School, Oprah was popular among both black and white students. She was elected a leader of the Student Council. She was selected to attend the White House Conference on Youth, as one of the two representatives chosen from Tennessee because of their academic and leadership abilities. And, she won the Miss Fire Prevention contest in Nashville, the first black woman to win the event. Finally, it seemed, Oprah Winfrey was experiencing her greatest potential.

3

A Professional Woman

Oprah Winfrey once claimed that she started her broadcasting career because she was bored at home after her father and stepmother restricted her to only one hour of television a day. "I hated that," she once told a reporter, "but it is the absolute reason I got my first job in radio."

When she was only 17 years old, Oprah became a newsreader at WVOL radio in Nashville. The year was 1971, and Oprah knew some of the people at the radio station because a disc jockey had interviewed her after she returned from the White House conference. The people at the radio station had also encouraged Oprah to enter the Miss Fire Prevention contest. They thought that Oprah sounded almost like a professional broadcaster when they heard her taped voice.

Oprah was thrilled by the idea of working at WVOL. Every day after school she went to the radio station and worked for several hours. After she graduated from East High School, she chose to attend Tennessee State University in Nashville, a historically African-American college, while she continued her work at the radio station and lived at home.

In 1972, Oprah won the Miss Black Nashville contest, and soon after, she went on to win the Miss Black Tennessee pageant. It wasn't long before a television station in town called Oprah and asked her to audition for a position. At first, Oprah turned the station down. But when the station manager called back a few more times, she decided to do it while she continued studying at Tennessee State. Oprah accepted a full-time job as a weekend news co-anchor at WTVF-TV. At 19, she was the youngest anchor for the Nashville news, as well as the city's first woman and the first African-American anchor. She had no television experience. "I had no idea what to do," Oprah said in an interview, "so I pretended to be Barbara Walters."

During her time at WTVF-TV, Oprah learned a great deal about television broadcasting. Although she had thought about becoming an actress, Oprah decided to pursue a broadcasting career instead of completing her college degree. Soon, the manager at a television station in Baltimore, Maryland, called.

BALTIMORE BECKONS

In August 1976, 22-year-old Oprah Winfrey began working for WJZ-TV in Baltimore as a news anchor and reporter. She was perfectly comfortable in front of the camera, although her relaxed style took some people by surprise. They weren't used to news anchors who laughed at their mistakes or cried during sad stories. One of the news stories was especially tragic—seven children were killed in a house fire. Winfrey cried with their mother while she tried to do the news report. Even though she had argued against doing the interview on the air, her producer decided to run it. Some people at WJZ thought that Winfrey was unprofessional for not remaining impartial during the news story, as reporters are taught to do.

While Winfrey was struggling to hide her emotions, she also encountered several other challenges in her new job. Her bosses in Baltimore thought that she did not look quite right. They sent her to a famous designer for a wardrobe consultation. Then, they sent her to New York for a makeover because they said her hair was too thick. Her hair was thinned out, but Winfrey was embarrassed by the way she looked. It was years before she let another hairdresser touch her head. The managers at the Baltimore station even sent her to a voice coach, who told her that her voice was fine but that she was too nice on the air. Winfrey didn't understand—she had been taught to be a nice person all of her life. Now, all of a sudden, she wasn't supposed to be nice anymore. This was a low point in Winfrey's Baltimore career. She was depressed. Each time after she finished a news show, Winfrey would go to the local mall and eat at the food court. Slowly, she began putting on weight.

Still, there were bright spots in Winfrey's life. Around this time, she met a woman who eventually became her best friend. Gayle King was a production assistant at WJZ. Winfrey and King had much in common—both were young, black women who had their whole careers ahead of them. But King's childhood had been very different from Winfrey's. She grew up in Chevy Chase, Maryland. Her father was an electronics engineer, and her mother stayed at home to take care of the family. One snowy night Winfrey invited King to stay overnight at her apartment instead of driving home on icy roads. The two women gabbed late into the night. "It was like being a 13-year-old and going over to a friend's house and staying up all night talking," King once told a reporter. "We just gossiped about work and the station…"

Winfrey also made another friend while working in Baltimore. Maria Shriver, who worked at WJZ at the time, was the niece of President John F. Kennedy. Years later, Winfrey

Gayle King is pictured here at the premiere of the film *Beloved*, which starred Oprah Winfrey. King and Winfrey have been best friends since working at WJZ-TV in Baltimore in the mid-1970s. For a time in the 1990s, King also had a talk show of her own.

attended Shriver's elaborate wedding to Arnold Schwarzenegger at Hyannis, Massachusetts. Shriver asked Winfrey to read the poem, "How Do I Love Thee?" during the ceremony, and Winfrey was happy to do so for her friend.

Gayle King

Gayle King has been Oprah Winfrey's best friend ever since they stayed up late one night talking while they both were working at WJZ-TV, a Baltimore television station. King graduated from the University of Maryland with a degree in psychology, but she began a television career soon after that. She was a production assistant at WJZ while Winfrey was an anchor at the station. After leaving WJZ, King became a reporter-in-training at WTOP-TV in Washington, D.C., and then a reporter at WDAF-TV in Kansas City.

Next, King's career took her to Hartford, Connecticut, to work as an anchor for the evening news on WFSB-TV, a CBS affiliate. She worked in Hartford for 18 years until she left in 1999 to join Winfrey in her new magazine venture called *O, The Oprah Magazine*. During her time in Hartford, King had two forays into the national television market. She left briefly to co-host *Cover to Cover*, an NBC talk show, with Maury Povich in 1991. Then she hosted her own syndicated talk show, *The Gayle King Show*, which debuted in September 1997. The show was canceled within a year—King was on vacation with Winfrey in the Caribbean when the announcement was made. In her contract, King made sure that her show would never be on the air at the same time as *The Oprah Winfrey Show*. She joked that she was afraid of competition from her best friend, whom she talks with on the phone nearly every day. Despite styling her half-hour show on Winfrey's hour-long program, King didn't have the following that Winfrey has.

Just before the magazine's debut, King became the liaison between *O*'s staff in New York City and Winfrey, who is based in Chicago. As editor-at-large for *O*, King continues to oversee the magazine's content each month and has helped guide it toward becoming one of the widest-read magazines available today.

OFF THE NEWS DESK

Believing that she wasn't working out as a news anchor, Winfrey's bosses at WJZ kept trying to figure out what to do with her. After all, she had a six-year contract with the station so they knew they needed to fit her in somewhere. Just a few months after moving to town, she was taken off the news anchor desk. A new general manager for the station had arrived, and he decided that Winfrey should be the host of a

Baltimore-focused morning talk show. Along with Richard Sher, she became the co-host of a local show, *People Are Talking*. That was when Winfrey realized that she had found her true talent. Winfrey asked questions, listened carefully as her guests answered, and asked the next question based on her guests' answers. Her style seemed to click with Sher's style, even though he was a more traditional broadcaster, asking each guest a predetermined list of questions. Winfrey discovered her strength—she worked best in a talk show format.

Interestingly, *People Are Talking* was on the air at the same time as a popular, nationally syndicated talk show, hosted by a silver-haired man named Phil Donahue. People in Baltimore had to choose between watching Donahue or *People Are Talking*. Even though Donahue was popular across the country, the folks in Baltimore started tuning in to Winfrey and Sher. The producers at WJZ didn't ignore that fact. They were thrilled.

Even though she seemed to be a success on the air, Winfrey still had some challenges in her personal life. Her boyfriend moved away, and she was lonely. She continued to gain weight. Winfrey soon fell in love with a man she thought was special. Unfortunately, he was married, and that relationship didn't work out either. Winfrey became very depressed. She is an optimist, though. Even when times are tough, she looks ahead to better days. And that is what she did in Baltimore.

In the meantime, she also became better at her job. All of Winfrey's experiences—from her poor childhood to the abuse that occurred during her teen years to these failed relationships—made Winfrey a better talk show host. She could talk to her show's guests about many topics because she had experienced them, too. Although it might make some people nervous, Winfrey seemed to thrive in front of the camera with a live audience watching all that she did. In fact, Winfrey seemed to be more energetic and more curious in front of a live audience.

While living in Baltimore, Oprah bought a book by Pulitzer Prize-winning author Alice Walker. It was titled *The Color*

Purple. Winfrey liked the book's theme about abused and mistreated women rising above their misfortunes. In fact, she admired the book so much that she bought several copies and

Author Alice Walker greeted photographers on opening night of *The Color Purple,* the Broadway musical based on her novel and produced by Oprah Winfrey. Winfrey became a fan of the book in the 1970s and bought copies to pass out to her friends. Winfrey would have many connections with the book in the coming years.

passed them out to her friends. Little did Winfrey know at the time just how much influence *The Color Purple* would have on her life.

Other events in Baltimore also helped to shape Winfrey's life. During one of her shows, Winfrey first realized that being sexually assaulted was never her fault. She had only been in Baltimore for a few years when she was interviewing someone who had been sexually abused. She came to see that many other people had lived with the same pain. That was the beginning of what has been Winfrey's career-long drive to help children who are in dangerous situations.

A few years later, in the middle of another interview, in true Oprah Winfrey fashion, the talk show host responded to something her guest said by announcing that she also had been sexually abused. Winfrey's guest cried, and so did Winfrey. Viewers were astonished. Many other people called the station to say that they, too, had been sexually abused as youngsters.

Instead of just talking about subjects that were important in Baltimore, Winfrey began tackling universal topics—love, abuse, divorce, suicide, family finances, and similar personal matters. Winfrey began to search for new and interesting topics, as did other talk show hosts around the country. But, somehow, Winfrey made viewers feel as if she were their best friend. Her audience continued to grow.

The team of Oprah Winfrey and Richard Sher became a fast success in Baltimore. Soon they were approached to syndicate their program, which meant that television viewers in other cities could also watch the show.

Winfrey and Sher agreed to a syndication deal and signed a contract stating that they would get $10,000 per city after 50 cities signed up to air *People Are Talking*. Only 12 cities ever showed *People Are Talking*, though. Too many topics on the program were still focused on Baltimore, and Winfrey was beginning to think that she could do an even better job if she worked alone rather than with a co-host.

4

Chicago Loves Oprah

Oprah Winfrey had been in Baltimore for about seven years when one of her show's producers left to become a producer at WLS-TV, a station in Chicago. It did not take long before Winfrey also began looking around for other jobs. By this time, she knew she could host a television talk show by herself, and she was interested in trying. "I'm grateful to Baltimore because of all I learned there and the chance to develop my confidence," she once told a reporter, "but I didn't really blossom until I went on my own and was free to be myself."

Eventually, Winfrey had the opportunity to audition for a program called *A.M. Chicago*, which was not doing well in the local ratings. *A.M. Chicago* was ranked third behind two more popular television shows, including Phil Donahue's program. Winfrey was nervous about her audition tape, and she stayed awake nearly all night to try to make a good one. In the end, her audition went well and, before she knew it, she was offered the host's job on *A.M. Chicago.*

When Winfrey announced that she was leaving Baltimore for the bigger Midwestern city of Chicago, she didn't receive much support. Some people told her that the job would not work out because she was an overweight, black woman. She didn't look like any other person who had ever hosted a television talk show before, and while she may have been a success in Baltimore, some wondered if a black host could make it in Chicago. The year was 1983, and the Windy City was coming out of a period of riots and racial tension. Winfrey's best friend, Gayle King, was one of the few people who supported her move.

The WLS station manager offered Winfrey around $200,000 a year to work on the show. The salary was much more than she was earning in Baltimore. At age 29, Winfrey started her new job in January 1984. She was excited about the job, but she was also nervous. Many people told her that it would be diffi-cult to compete against Phil Donahue. Winfrey was not sure if she made the right choice for her career, but she loved Chicago. Immediately, she settled down and felt as if the city was where she was always supposed to be. Winfrey liked the idea of working solo because it gave her a chance to be herself without having to worry about her co-host's response. She was known to kick off her shoes while on the air and get comfort-able while she talked.

Because of her weight gain in Baltimore, Winfrey had already tried a variety of diets. But she could never lose much weight. "I think weight has been a way of sheltering my own sense of power," she once told a reporter for *The Washington Post.* "It makes people more comfortable with me and in many ways me more comfortable with other people."

When she got to Chicago, Winfrey was heavier than she had ever been. She once said she gained 10 pounds during her first week in the city because she was so nervous about the new show. Winfrey knew that few talk show hosts were overweight, and she worried about that. "Eating has been my way of saying, 'Well, if I fail, it's because of the weight, it's because I'm fat,'" she said.

Through the cold winter days of her early Chicago success, Winfrey celebrated with more food. She was at a boxing match to watch Mike Tyson fight when she realized that she and the boxer had something in common: They both weighed 216 pounds. It was then that Winfrey realized that she had a serious problem. She was up to 221 pounds before she decided to go on a serious diet.

A SUCCESS FROM THE START

Meanwhile, Winfrey's show did not fail at all. The first month she was in town, *A.M. Chicago* became the top-rated program in the area. "I like Phil Donahue," Winfrey once told a writer for *Ladies' Home Journal.* "But I have to admit, it feels good to beat him."

Winfrey was outdrawing the successful Donahue, and many people seemed to understand why. She was personable when she talked to people on the show. She didn't hesitate to touch or hug them while doing an interview. She seemed as if she was really listening to them and responding to what they said. Women of all colors, and many men, felt as if Winfrey was a good friend. "She's like the one friend you trust," a fan once told a reporter for the *Los Angeles Times.* "You stick with a girlfriend like that, you know."

Still, Winfrey was fighting the urge to eat continually. She even sponsored a "Diet With Oprah" segment during her show. As Winfrey's first year in Chicago came to an end, *A.M. Chicago's* name was changed. It became *The Oprah Winfrey Show,* and the station allotted an hour for it. She thought she would enjoy working in front of a live audience, so the station agreed to allow a few people into the studio to watch the show. Winfrey would stop by a doughnut shop so that audience members had a treat after the show.

Oprah Winfrey left Baltimore to become the host of *A.M. Chicago* in January 1984. Here, Winfrey tries on a pair of cowboy boots during a segment of her show in 1985.

Chicago did, in fact, seem to be the place for Winfrey. By the end of 1984, it appeared as if everyone was talking about her. *Chicago* magazine did an article about her phenomenal rise to the top, and the *Chicago Tribune* television critic lauded her style as a host. She was mentioned as one of Chicago's hottest stars by *Newsweek* magazine. Just a few weeks later, late-night talk show host Johnny Carson invited her to appear on *The Tonight Show*.

FROM TV TO MOVIES

Events began to move very quickly in Winfrey's life. Before she knew it, she was auditioning for a movie role. One of the film's producers, Quincy Jones, had seen Winfrey on television when he was in Chicago, and he asked the casting company to give her a call. Because Winfrey had really wanted to be an actress when she was in college, she saw this as a huge opportunity. In fact, ever since she had read Alice Walker's book in Baltimore, she had wanted to play a part in the movie based on Walker's novel. "*The Color Purple* for me was a fantasy, an obsession. It was a part of my greatest heart's desire," she said when she was interviewed for the DVD version of the movie.

When Winfrey got the call, though, the person from the casting company said she was being asked to audition for a movie called *Moon Song*. Winfrey had trouble believing that— she had never heard of the movie. But she decided to go to the audition anyway. It was a bitter cold Chicago day when she went to the reading. She knew the film was *The Color Purple* the minute she saw the script. But, for at least a couple of months, Winfrey waited. No call came. She thought she did not get the part, so she went to a health spa in California: It was time to focus on getting into shape. Winfrey remembers that she was crying, running around the track at the spa one day when someone called her to the phone. "I was told, 'If you lose a pound, you could lose a part,'" she recalled referring to the body shape required for the role. Winfrey had won the part she had always desired. She left the spa and stopped at Dairy Queen to guarantee that she stayed plump.

The movie offer, though, posed another dilemma for Winfrey—how could she be an actress and still host her show? Winfrey was determined that she could do both—she would be in the film and continue her successful Chicago show at the same time. It took weeks for Winfrey to negotiate a deal with her Chicago television station and the movie producers. The movie would require Winfrey to work in Hollywood, California, and North Carolina for several weeks. At first, the television station managers did not want her to be away for so long. Finally, a deal was reached. All the people involved recognized that Winfrey could do both jobs and be quite successful, too.

In *The Color Purple*, Winfrey played Sofia, who was married to a man named Harpo. (Interestingly, just a few years later Oprah named her production company Harpo, which is also her name spelled backward.) The movie also starred Whoopi Goldberg and was directed by Steven Spielberg.

Oprah Winfrey made her movie debut in 1985 playing Sofia in *The Color Purple,* directed by Steven Spielberg. Her portrayal earned her an Academy Award nomination for best supporting actress.

The Academy Awards

The Academy Awards have been given out since the first ceremony was held on May 16, 1929, at the Hollywood Roosevelt Hotel. Back then, 250 people attended—a far cry from the masses of stars and celebrities who now go to the annual event each spring in Los Angeles.

People who win Academy Awards receive a bronze statue of a knight holding a crusader's sword and standing on a reel of film. The statue was designed in 1928 by MGM's chief art director Cedric Gibbons, and today it weighs 8.5 pounds and is 13.5 inches tall. Although the award is frequently called the Oscar, no one knows the exact origin of the name. Some people believe the statue was named years ago after an uncle of one of the executive directors of the Academy of Motion Picture Arts and Sciences. Through time, Oscar's look has occasionally changed, and it has been presented in a variety of forms to some recipients. The ventriloquist Edgar Bergen was once given a wooden Oscar, and Walt Disney was honored with a full-size Oscar and seven miniature statues for his animated work, *Snow White and the Seven Dwarfs*.

The idea for giving the Academy Awards came from the Academy of Motion Picture Arts and Sciences, an honorary organization that today consists of 6,000 motion picture artists and craftsmen. The first black actor to win an Oscar for best actor was Sidney Poitier for the role of Homer Smith in *Lilies of the Field* in 1963, and the first black woman to win best actress was Halle Berry for the part of Leticia Musgrove in *Monster's Ball* in 2001. The first African-American performer to win an Oscar was Hattie McDaniel, who was named best supporting actress for 1939's *Gone With the Wind*.

The Academy was formed in 1927 with only 36 members, including production executives and film stars. The organization's original mission was clear—it would advance the arts and sciences of motion pictures. That is why the Academy honors not only movie stars, but also the people behind the scenes responsible for everything from the sound to the cinematography to the costumes in a movie.

The first movies with sound were produced just before the first Academy Awards were handed out. For the first 15 years, the ceremony was held during a banquet at Hollywood-area hotels. During World War II, the sixteenth-annual awards moved to Grauman's Chinese Theatre and the program was broadcast overseas to American military men and women. (The Hollywood Walk of Fame is in front of Grauman's Chinese Theatre.) The Academy Awards were first presented on television in 1953. Through the years, the Academy Awards have been held in several Los Angeles-area venues, but the ceremony has been staged at the Kodak Theater, just steps away from Grauman's Chinese Theatre, since 2001.

One of the most startling moments in the movie came at the end, when Winfrey surprised the cast and crew by ad-libbing some poignant lines about the historical role of black women. When *The Color Purple* premiered in December 1985, Winfrey received rave reviews for her portrayal of Sofia. Since she had always wanted to be an actress, she was pleased to have made her movie debut in such an important film. Although critics praised the film, black men in several cities protested the way they were portrayed on screen. A few months after *The Color Purple* opened, Winfrey was nominated for an Academy Award for best supporting actress. Before she left for the awards ceremony, a Chicago movie critic told her she wouldn't win.

Still, despite her film success, Winfrey wasn't completely happy with herself. She remained overweight. When she went to the Academy Awards, she was probably the heaviest she had ever been. In fact, the dress she had especially designed for that evening was too tight, and she was afraid it would split if she were called on stage. Winfrey did not have to worry, however, because she did not win the award. The movie critic was right. Although Winfrey did not receive an Academy Award, her experience in *The Color Purple* convinced her that she wanted to continue acting.

IN DEMAND

Winfrey was becoming a busy and popular woman. She was invited to many places to speak. People seemed to listen to every word she had to say. She had a part in another film called *Native Son,* which was being filmed in Chicago. The film was based on Richard Wright's famous novel of the same name. Winfrey portrayed a mother whose son killed a white woman in the 1940s. Although she earned positive reviews for her work in *Native Son,* the film was considered mediocre compared with *The Color Purple.*

Despite her career success, personal happiness still seemed to elude Winfrey. Her weight was still troublesome to her. It would take Winfrey many years to realize that her weight issue was about many things that had affected her life. "My greatest failure was in believing that the weight issue was just about weight," she told a reporter for *People* magazine. "It's not. It's about not being able to say no. It's about not handling stress properly. It's about sexual abuse. It's about all the things that cause other people to become alcoholics and drug addicts." Winfrey would spend much of her life learning how to handle the challenges of her weight.

5

National Exposure

It was a warm September afternoon in 1986, and celebration was in the air. Oprah Winfrey and her show's staff gathered in Grant Park in Chicago to have lunch and celebrate the successful coast-to-coast launch of *The Oprah Winfrey Show*. Employees from WLS attended, as did officials from King World Productions, Inc., the company responsible for distributing Winfrey's show around the world.

The Oprah Winfrey Show had been booming in Chicago when two brothers, Roger and Michael King, approached Winfrey about syndication. The brothers were the owners of King World Productions, Inc. Even though other syndicators were talking to Winfrey about taking the show to stations across the country, Winfrey and her business advisor decided that the King brothers could do the job.

The night before syndication was to begin, Winfrey was filled with doubt. She wondered what effects the move would have. She was excited, but nervous. "I keep wondering how my life will change…," she wrote in her journal. It would have been difficult for Winfrey to realize at that time just how much her life would change.

On September 8, 1986, *The Oprah Winfrey Show* became a national program, shown on 138 television stations. Because few people outside of Chicago had ever heard of Oprah Winfrey, it was difficult for her to find guests for the show. She and her staff decided that the first national show would be about how to find a man. She also did a show that week about neo-Nazis and women who had been raped by their doctors. The audience seemed to love her. Soon, nearly 200 stations were broadcasting the program, and Winfrey was talking to millions of people Mondays to Fridays each week. The King brothers were right—Winfrey was a tremendous success.

On the rainy morning of December 14, 1986, Winfrey's father opened his barbershop in Nashville and talked to Jill Nelson, a reporter from *The Washington Post*, who was visiting his shop. The barbershop was small and cluttered with magazines and many other items. A poster announcing a local appearance by Oprah Winfrey was hanging in a corner. The reporter wanted to be there while Vernon Winfrey watched his daughter's show. The topic that day was child abuse.

"I never knew," Vernon Winfrey told the reporter, "at the time Oprah came to live with me, that had ever happened to her. If we had known, we might have handled her a little bit differently, not knowing what kind of stress she was going through." Vernon Winfrey said that he was proud to see his daughter addressing these difficult issues during her television program.

By 1986, Vernon Winfrey was an established personality around Nashville. He was a city councilman and a deacon in his church, the Faith-United Missionary Baptist Church, where Oprah had quoted Scripture and sang when she was a teenager. Besides being a barber, he still owned the small grocery store that he had when Oprah lived with him as a teenager. Vernon Winfrey beamed when his grown-up 32-year-old daughter appeared on television that day. "You know," he told the reporter, "Oprah's show has caused me to lose some money between 9 and 10 in the morning."

Oprah Winfrey was making headlines around the country. In Washington, D.C., there was a firestorm when another black, female talk show host lost her program because Winfrey's show was being broadcast at the same time. Winfrey responded that television was a competitive business. She knew that people at stations around the country were losing their jobs because her syndicated show had come into their areas, but there wasn't much Winfrey thought she could do about the situation.

A NEW RELATIONSHIP

While her popularity continued to grow, so did her interest in Stedman Graham. A former basketball player, Graham was a tall, handsome man with a master's degree in education. He had grown up in Whitesboro, a small New Jersey town, and was one of six children. As a youngster, he worked alongside his father, who was a carpenter and painter. His mother was a nurse's assistant. Graham had also struggled with his heritage—Whitesboro was nearly all black, surrounded by areas that were all white. When he was young, Graham thought the color of his skin would predetermine his goals. But—much like Winfrey—as he grew into adulthood, he realized he had the freedom to accomplish a great deal. When Winfrey met Graham, he ran a drug-counseling program called Athletes Against Drugs.

Graham and Winfrey had briefly met at several social events, and soon he began pursuing her. But Winfrey and her protective staff at the television station were suspicious. She was a well-known talk show host, and she was still overweight. Winfrey and her staff were worried that Graham was only interested in her money. Finally, Winfrey agreed to go to

Oprah Winfrey attended a party before the Mike Tyson–Michael Spinks fight in Atlantic City in 1988 along with her father, Vernon Winfrey (left) and her boyfriend, Stedman Graham.

dinner with Graham, and they had a good time. The two started going out more frequently, and Winfrey found that she really liked Graham.

But their relationship had a rather bumpy beginning. Winfrey's feelings about Graham weren't private at all. She shared the travails of her relationship with the millions of people who watched her program every day. Graham struggled with the fact that he was dating a wealthy and popular talk show host. Eventually, Graham moved back to High Point, North Carolina, where his public relations firm was based, while he and Winfrey continued a long-distance relationship.

In the meantime, Winfrey was reading articles about herself that she didn't really believe. "I remember reading in the first year I was syndicated that I was going to make $11 million that year, and I'm like, 'Well, I don't know what they're talking about,'" Winfrey once told a reporter. But the syndication contract with the King brothers was generous. In fact, Winfrey said that she ended up making more than $11 million that first year. That was quite a pay raise from the $200,000 that the television station had paid her to move to Chicago. Suddenly, Winfrey was a very wealthy woman.

"I remember the first million-dollar check that came in," Winfrey once told a reporter. "Somewhere there's a picture of me holding the check, me and Gayle [King]. And we were just like, 'Oh my God, it's a million dollars!'"

TACKLING TOUGH ISSUES

Meanwhile, Winfrey's popularity continued to grow. In those years, her television program was categorized with other shows that did confrontational interviews. Winfrey thought it was necessary to expose some people and to be more confrontational on her program. For one episode, she even went to all-white Forsyth County, Georgia, where blacks had not lived since 1912, when the black population was driven from the county after a crime had been committed against a white teenage girl. Winfrey insisted that the audience be only local residents; therefore, only white people were in the audience. Outside, black activists protested and said that Winfrey was not hearing their point of view. Winfrey said that she simply wanted to find out why the white people of Forsyth County did not want black people living near them. Her ultimate goal was to get the residents of the county to reconsider their beliefs.

Winfrey liked to tie her show's programming to current events, too. Another show Winfrey did that year was about a very touching topic. She invited family members of the crew of the *Challenger* to talk about their relatives who had died when the space shuttle exploded in January 1986. This period was an amazing time for Winfrey. She was making an impact on many people's lives.

In the meantime, her life was also quickly changing. She could hardly believe the amount of money she was making or the idea that she could buy whatever she wanted. Winfrey bought a condominium with a wonderful view of Lake Michigan. This luxury high-rise in Chicago was quite different from her grandparents' farm in Mississippi or the crowded apartments her mother had in Milwaukee. Winfrey had her new condominium designed with white walls and floors, white rugs with silver threads, and overstuffed white sofas. Months later, Winfrey insisted that her mother retire from her job as a dietitian at a hospital, and she bought her a condominium in Milwaukee. Winfrey also promised her mother $5,000 a month for the rest of her life.

Winfrey finally got her diploma from Tennessee State University in the spring of 1987. Because she had left the college when she went to work in Baltimore, Winfrey had never fulfilled her wish—or her father's desire—that she get a college degree. In fact, every time she visited her father in Nashville, he would remind her that she would never amount to anything

On her talk show, Oprah Winfrey is known for her connection with the guests and with audience members. "She's like the one friend you trust," a fan said.

without a college degree. After Winfrey finished a project that fulfilled a requirement in a media course at Tennessee State, she was told that she would finally graduate. She was asked to be the guest speaker at Tennessee State's commencement ceremony. "Even though I've done a few things with my life, every time I've come home, my father said, 'You need that degree,'" she told the audience. "So this is a special day for my dad." Then, Winfrey announced that she would establish a scholarship program in her father's name at the school for others who needed help. Her father watched proudly from the audience.

In December, Winfrey took her staff to New York City for a shopping spree. Her staff had no more than six people, and Winfrey genuinely appreciated the hard work that they did. She treated them like her family, bringing cookies to work, buying sweaters for them if she ran across a sale, and going out with her staff members after the long work day ended.

As Winfrey's popularity grew in Chicago, she was invited to many benefits and charity events. One of her assistants, Billy Rizzo, had AIDS, and Winfrey was quite saddened by it. She encouraged the audience at an AIDS fundraiser in Chicago to support funding for AIDS research. At that time, AIDS was a fairly new disease, and medical advances were few. Rizzo died the following year, and Winfrey's half-brother, Jeffrey Lee, died of AIDS the year after that.

ACCLAIM AND MORE ACCLAIM

Winfrey spoke at many similar events even though her popularity was soaring and her workload was heavy. Her hard work paid off, though. In 1987, she won her first Emmy Award as outstanding talk show host. *The Oprah Winfrey Show* was named outstanding talk/service show. The following year, Winfrey became the youngest winner of the Broadcaster of the Year Award given by the International Radio and Television Society. The National Conference of Christians and Jews gave her its Humanitarian Award. In 1989, Gloria Steinem, the editor of *Ms.*, presented Winfrey with the magazine's Woman of the Year award for being a role model for all women. "Those who preceded Oprah were yesterday's pathfinders, and today Oprah Winfrey continues her journey, paving the way for other young white, black, Hispanic, Asian, and Native American women to follow," wrote Maya Angelou in a tribute published in *Ms.* "She is one of our Roadmakers." Later that year,

Maya Angelou

When Oprah Winfrey hosted her Legends Luncheon in the spring of 2005, Dr. Maya Angelou was seated at her right hand during the photo session for *O* magazine. Winfrey has long said that Maya Angelou is one of her greatest mentors in life, and Angelou has frequently been a guest on *The Oprah Winfrey Show*.

Maya Angelou was born Marguerite Ann Johnson on April 4, 1928, in St. Louis, Missouri. She was the daughter of Bailey Johnson, a doorman and naval dietitian, and Vivian Baxter Johnson, a registered nurse. As a girl, Angelou attended public schools in Arkansas and California. She studied music, dance, and drama through the years and has had a thriving career as an author, poet, playwright, and more. Angelou is the mother of one son; the motherhood theme is apparent in the six books of her autobiographical series. The series starts with *I Know Why the Caged Bird Sings*, which was published in 1970 and received a nomination for the National Book Award.

In late 1992, President-elect Bill Clinton asked her to write and read a poem for his inauguration, the first inaugural poem in 32 years. She wrote "On the Pulse of Morning" for the special event and talked of racial and religious harmony and peace for people of all origins.

Angelou has overcome adversity in her life after facing racism from whites and being treated poorly by many men. Her life has had many turns, from being a young teenage mother to being a prostitute to the kidnapping of her son. Instead of succumbing to these challenges, Angelou studied hard and turned to the arts to express her frustrations and feelings. She spent years documenting her life, including her travels to Africa and Europe, and her work as an artist and a civil-rights activist. She worked with Malcolm X and the Rev. Dr. Martin Luther King, Jr. Her articles, essays, stories, and poems are widely published, and she has received hundreds of awards.

Winfrey and Graham were invited to a White House state dinner given by President George H.W. Bush. Indeed, it seemed as if Winfrey was making an impact.

Winfrey, still, tried to find personal happiness. Her relationship with Graham continued, but she remained unhappy with her weight. She once spent four months drinking only a diet milkshake each day, and she lost 67 pounds. She took up jogging to try to get into better shape. On one of her shows, she pulled a little red wagon that was filled with 67 pounds of fat onto the stage, while she showed off the size-10 Calvin Klein jeans that she wore. "I got down to 145 pounds and stayed there for one day before the regaining began," she said several years later in O, The Oprah Magazine.

Meanwhile, Winfrey's movie career continued. Commuting to Hollywood, she started work on a television mini-series called The Women of Brewster Place, which was about seven black women who lived in the same apartment building. Professionally, Winfrey made an important decision in 1988. She needed to have more control of her television program so she could continue doing movies. Her contract with King World Productions and the television station was supposed to continue until 1991. During negotiations, Winfrey agreed to do the program until at least 1993. But she set up a company called Harpo Productions, and after many months of negotiations by her attorney, who was also her business advisor, Harpo gained control of The Oprah Winfrey Show. Establishing Harpo Productions and taking control of her show was the first of many business decisions that would add to Winfrey's power and influence around the world.

BRANCHING OUT

It was time that Winfrey got more serious about her business. She bought a huge production facility in Chicago that she named Harpo Studios. She also bought herself a serene farm in the Indiana countryside—a place where she could escape the city and

For years, Oprah Winfrey has struggled with her weight. In 1988, she lost 67 pounds in four months by drinking only a diet milkshake each day. To show how much she lost, she wheeled 67 pounds of fat on a toy wagon onto her set, shown above. "I got down to 145 pounds and stayed there for one day before the regaining began," she said several years later.

relax on weekends. By establishing Harpo Studios, Winfrey became the first black woman to own a major production company and only the third woman in history to accomplish that goal. In the next few years, Winfrey focused on producing other films that featured the experiences of black people.

She purchased the rights to the Toni Morrison novel *Beloved*, which was about a black woman who sees the ghosts of slavery. Although the movie would not be made for several more years, Winfrey went to great lengths to understand the role of Sethe, the character of the mother, whom she portrayed in the movie. She went into the Maryland woods and tried to run the path of the Underground Railroad in her bare feet. "I needed to know what it felt like to be out in the wilderness, barefoot and lost," she told a writer for *Good Housekeeping* just before the movie was released in 1998. She also tried to live the life of a slave, hoeing and pulling weeds while an actor who played a slave master yelled at her. One day she could not take it anymore. She broke down and sobbed. Through this torturous exercise, Winfrey finally understood the life of Sethe and was able to portray her in the movie.

Winfrey also bought the rights to other literary works, and as another business sideline, she became a partner in a Chicago restaurant called the Eccentric. The restaurant lasted six years.

Throughout the workweek, Winfrey and her staff continued to put in many hours to make *The Oprah Winfrey Show* a success. It wasn't unusual for this small group to be together for 15 hours a day. Winfrey addressed many topics that previous talk show hosts had avoided: menopause, Satanism, pornography, lesbianism, and the sexual exploitation of children. But she included lighter topics, too—like interviews with Robin Williams, the cast of the television series *L.A. Law*, and others in the Hollywood limelight.

Some of Winfrey's riskier topics, though, began to get more national attention. An organization was formed in Detroit called "Americans for Responsible Television," partly in reaction to shows that Winfrey had done. Meanwhile, other daytime talk show hosts—like Geraldo Rivera, Sally Jessy Raphaël, and Phil Donahue—were addressing similar topics. The popularity of these talk shows partly led to the birth of a string of evening news programs such as *Primetime Live*.

Winfrey and her staff spent many hours looking at possible topics for the show. They read news clippings and did other research. They had plenty of discussions, and they made many telephone calls to people they thought would be good subjects for the program. Eventually, they always came up with the right mix of guests in order to present a program on a particular topic. They were proud of their work. "For many of the years," Winfrey said, "I thought my staff was beleaguered and was overworked and burning themselves out."

When she appeared on Johnny Carson's *Tonight Show*, Winfrey was stunned to discover a staff of 40 people hard at work. So, she decided that *The Oprah Winfrey Show* would add a few more staff members. Still, people worked hard, and some left the program because they were so tired. Others were young and enthusiastic and joined Winfrey with no idea that the show would grow even more popular in the coming years.

6

Angels at Work

Oprah Winfrey's childhood seemed to influence her work greatly. The subjects of child abuse, neglect, and exploitation have all been discussed on her show. "We want parents to understand that all children … are at risk," Winfrey said during one of her programs. "We want parents to know that most offenders are people your child and you probably know—people that you know, people that you trust, and maybe even love, men like these."

While Winfrey spoke, it seemed as if she was thinking about her own childhood and the abuse she had suffered. In 1991, Winfrey was stunned to learn about the death of a four-year-old Chicago girl who had been molested and strangled. The girl's body was dumped into Lake Michigan. Winfrey had had enough. She considered her position of power and decided to try to take action regarding this issue. On November 12, 1991, she testified before the U.S. Senate Judiciary Committee to propose a new law that her attorneys had written. Winfrey implored the committee chair, Senator Joseph Biden, a Democrat from Delaware, to sponsor the bill in the U.S. Congress.

The man who was convicted of killing the four-year-old child was a known criminal who had previously been arrested for sexually abusing children. In proposing the law, Winfrey wanted to establish a national database of known sexual offenders. "You lose your childhood when you've been abused," Winfrey told the Senate Judiciary Committee. "My heart goes out to those children who are abused at home and have no one to turn to."

After she testified, Winfrey held a press conference and discussed her own sexual abuse by adult relatives and friends from the time she was 9 years old until she was 14. Winfrey

With Oprah Winfrey in attendance, President Bill Clinton signed the National Child Protection Act of 1993 into law. Winfrey was an ardent supporter of the legislation. Her attorneys helped to write the bill, and she testified before members of Congress in favor of it. The law created a database of known sexual offenders.

knew how those experiences had affected her self-esteem and led to her teenage promiscuity. She thought it was time to help children in similar situations. It took two years for Winfrey's proposal to become law. In 1993, President Bill Clinton signed the National Child Protection Act into law with Winfrey standing at his side. Her work on the legislation marked one of the first times that Winfrey went beyond her role as a talk show host to take on a problem in society. Once again, Winfrey proved that she had the power and influence to make things happen.

THE BOOK CLUB

On a professional level, Winfrey's popularity continued to skyrocket. In 1993, 1994, and 1995, she won Emmy Awards for outstanding talk show host. In 1994 and 1995, her program won the Emmy for outstanding talk/service show. Meanwhile, Winfrey began to re-examine the content of her show. She started to focus more on self-improvement and less on scandals. In 1996, she created Oprah's Book Club, reaching millions of people who hadn't read a book in years. The love of reading instilled in her by her father and stepmother had never disappeared, even though Winfrey was very busy and successful. She decided to feature one book a month on her program and to offer a small discussion during one episode, usually involving the book's author and some readers. Some authors were famous, like Toni Morrison; others weren't so well-known.

One day, Robert Morgan, an English professor at Cornell University, received a phone call from a woman who didn't identify herself. She had read his book, *Gap Creek*, and she wanted to use it for her book club. The professor thought it was a crank caller when the woman identified herself as Oprah Winfrey. In fact, the professor's book was featured on the show in January 2000 and, as a result, sold at least 650,000 copies— many more than it would have sold without Winfrey's endorsement. Morgan received letters from fans around the world, including people in Denmark, Australia, and Germany.

Morgan's case wasn't unusual, though. Winfrey's interest in books made many authors and their publishers wealthy. Both large and small publishers, known and new authors, began pursuing Winfrey—everyone wanted his or her book featured on her show. Being on *The Oprah Winfrey Show* was the formula for instant success. Sadly, in the year that Winfrey began her book club, one of her earliest reading influences, her stepmother Zelma Winfrey, died. Winfrey's life, as usual, had many ups and downs. That was also the year that Winfrey received one of the most prestigious awards in television, the George Foster Peabody Individual Achievement Award. Two years later, Winfrey received the National Academy of Television Arts and Sciences Lifetime Achievement Award.

CATTLE FARMERS' LAWSUIT

Certainly, Winfrey's life was far from perfect. In the usual style she used to talk about world issues and problems, Winfrey tackled the subject of "dangerous food" during her show on April 16, 1996. Winfrey was talking with Howard Lyman, a program director for the Humane Society of the United States, about dangerous foods when they discussed mad cow disease, which had killed hundreds of cattle in England. Lyman, a former cattle rancher who had become a vegetarian, said he feared that the disease would enter the United States. Winfrey responded that he had "just stopped me cold from ever eating another burger."

Her comment angered cattle farmers in Texas. After Winfrey made the statement, they claimed their business was severely affected. The farmers filed a $12 million lawsuit against Winfrey, saying that she made false and disparaging statements about the food. When the resulting trial began in January 1998 in Amarillo, Texas, Winfrey moved her daily show to that city. Winfrey felt strongly that as an American she had the right to free speech on her television show.

On the day that the jury was selected, animal-rights advocates wore cow suits to protest in front of the federal courthouse in Amarillo. The first day of the trial, Winfrey quietly entered the courtroom through a back door to avoid the hordes of fans crowded at the entrance. In the fashion of true entrepreneurship, Winfrey took advantage of being in Texas. Among others, her guests included actor Patrick Swayze and singer Clint Black—both natives of Texas. Despite the trial, many people in Amarillo loved having Winfrey's show in town, which she taped most evenings at the Amarillo Little Theatre. One Sunday, she attended Mount Zion Baptist Church. Another day, a woman reportedly handed her a résumé under the door of a restroom stall at the courthouse because she wanted to work for Winfrey.

At the time of the trial, no cases of mad cow disease had been reported in the United States. In fact, in 1989 the United States banned beef products from being imported from Great Britain. Great Britain and other parts of Europe had been dealing with mad cow disease for several years. The federal court jury ruled in Winfrey's favor, a decision that surprised her. She wept in the courtroom and then gave a statement to the press on the courthouse steps. She said, "Free speech not only lives, it rocks!" Although the cattle producers appealed the decision, Winfrey won the appeal in 2002, and the case was concluded.

Winfrey's focus on her program during the ongoing stress of the Amarillo trial proved how extraordinary her spirit was, and she continued to garner accolades. *Newsweek* magazine and *TV Guide* gave Winfrey special awards in 1997: *Newsweek* named her the "Most Important Person in Books and Media," and *TV Guide* called her the "Television Performer of the Year."

"Free speech not only lives, it rocks," Winfrey declared in February 1998 outside the federal courthouse in Amarillo, Texas. Cattlemen in Texas had filed a $12 million lawsuit against Winfrey in response to comments she made on her show. The federal jury ruled in her favor.

ON THE PERSONAL SIDE

Throughout the 1990s, though, Winfrey's personal life still seemed to be in a state of flux. She became engaged to Stedman Graham in 1992, but they could not seem to decide on a wedding date. A large New York publisher had given Winfrey a $4 million contract to write her autobiography, and Graham didn't want to get married at the same time that the book was released. Meanwhile, Winfrey was undergoing an intense process as she wrote the book, including a great deal of introspection as she peeled away the years back to her childhood. She discovered that, as a youngster, she desperately wanted love and attention. She examined her teenage promiscuity and, somehow, she realized that all of this pent-up need to be loved was related to her weight. The exercise of writing gave Winfrey the answers to many questions in her life. She had wanted to write a book that would inspire others, but instead Winfrey's book led her to a greater understanding of herself. The book she had written, however, was not one that she wanted others to read. In the end, she told her publisher that she did not want it printed.

Winfrey's weight still bothered her, but with this new understanding of herself, she decided to take action. At the time, in 1992, she had reached her highest weight: 237 pounds. She met an exercise physiologist named Bob Greene, whom she invited to move from Colorado to help her restructure her life. She wanted Greene to teach her to eat healthily and to create an exercise regime that kept her in good shape. He taught her that discipline came from willpower and that willpower came from the willingness to work hard. Greene jogged along Lake Michigan with Winfrey, and he worked out next to her at a gymnasium in the Harpo production facility.

By October 24, 1994, Winfrey was fit enough to run in the Marine Corps Marathon in Washington, D.C. She said it was one of the most fearless days of her life; getting herself into shape had taught her a great deal, including how not to be fearful. No longer was Winfrey afraid that she would make people angry or that she wasn't going to do or say the right thing. Winfrey finally felt mentally, and physically, healthy. Her relationship with Bob Greene, as his student, would continue for many years.

Meanwhile, Winfrey's relationships with the people who provided her support continued to grow stronger. In 1997, her friend Quincy Jones threw a party for her forty-third birthday at his home in Bel-Air, California. Steven Spielberg, who had directed *The Color Purple*; her friends Arnold Schwarzenegger

Oprah Winfrey ran with other participants in the Revlon Run/Walk for Women in Los Angeles in 1997. A few years before, she had begun a workout program with exercise physiologist Bob Greene. Her first marathon was the Marine Corps Marathon in 1994.

and Maria Shriver; actor Sidney Poitier; and others attended. Stedman Graham and Gayle King were there, too. Winfrey's life had definitely changed since she was a young girl who played by herself with a corncob doll her grandmother had made. Winfrey had many powerful and influential friends by the time she turned 43.

Graham and Winfrey agreed to appear on King's new talk show to chat about why they were still unmarried, despite being engaged since 1992. "We have a deep love and caring for each other and respect," Winfrey said during the show. "I say, it works so well the way it is, I wouldn't want to mess it up..." At times through the years, Winfrey also discussed why she had not had any children after giving birth as a teen. For years, she thought motherhood could be in her future, but the urge to have children never seemed to grow strong. Sometimes she even wondered if she was capable of being a good parent.

PEAKS AND VALLEYS

Although Winfrey's life seemed to be going well, disappointments still cropped up along the way. She had spent much energy during the filming of *Beloved*—even praying every morning in her trailer to the ancestors of slaves as she lit candles and read their names from historical documents she had collected. Winfrey and others involved in the film thought it could win an Academy Award. When the movie was released in 1998, however, she was disappointed that more people did not go to see it. Gayle King was with her in New York when they heard about the low box office figures for *Beloved*. The two women responded by eating big plates of macaroni and cheese.

Winfrey's popularity as a talk show host, though, was still soaring. *Time* magazine quantified her power and prestige when its editors named Winfrey as one of the 100 Most Influential People of the 20th Century in 1998. At the time, Winfrey had an estimated fortune of more than a half-billion dollars. Each day, about 14 million people in the United States watched her show, and that did not include the people in 120 other countries where the program was also on the air. In October 1998, Winfrey was honored to read a poem with her friend and mentor, Maya Angelou, at a ceremony in Washington, D.C., to honor Dorothy Height, who was president emerita of the National Council of Negro Women. Other speakers included influential people like the president's wife, Hillary Rodham Clinton, and the Rev. Jesse Jackson.

By 1999, it seemed that Winfrey was nearly embarrassed to have received so many awards through the years. She and her show had won 39 Daytime Emmy Awards, including 7 for outstanding host, 9 for outstanding talk show, and several for different creative elements that were involved in the show. Winfrey had also won an Emmy for producing an ABC Afterschool Special called *Shades of a Single Protein*. She asked that she be excluded from future Emmy competitions.

THE ANGEL NETWORK BEGINS

Despite all of the honor and praise, Winfrey was not yet satisfied. She wanted to use her and her show's influence to create some positive changes in the world. On September 18, 1997, Winfrey offered her viewers a challenge. She asked them to help her improve the lives of others by contributing to scholarships given through the Boys and Girls Clubs of America. She also asked viewers to consider volunteering their time with Habitat for Humanity to help build 200 homes for those in need.

"Oprah's challenge was just so powerful that within 24 hours I had faxed our commitment to sponsor a house to Habitat International," a businesswoman from Pittsburgh, Pennsylvania, later told a newspaper reporter. A Pittsburgh home was restored as a result of the woman's commitment of $60,000 and the volunteer work of 160 local residents who wanted to make a difference. Once again, Winfrey's challenge had been successful. More of her viewers met the challenge, too. In fact, their enthusiasm encouraged Winfrey to form a charity called Oprah's Angel Network the following year. Winfrey wanted to enable all people to reach their greatest potential. Starting with the formation of Oprah's Angel Network, Winfrey's viewers began donating thousands of dollars toward a huge range of projects around the world.

At one point, collection boxes were placed in cities around the country to collect money for college scholarships. Winfrey encouraged viewers to put their spare change into the boxes, and she promised that she would match the total amount given. The project became known as the world's largest piggy bank, and Winfrey promised to give one scholarship in every state. In St. Petersburg, Florida, viewers of her show complained in the local newspaper that the collection box was too far away—in a shopping center between Tampa and St. Petersburg. "It's a great idea...," the spokesman for the local television affiliate that aired *The Oprah Winfrey Show* told a reporter from the *St. Petersburg Times.* "It just may have grown larger

IN HER OWN WORDS...

Oprah Winfrey has long been an advocate for service to others, and for the holiday season of 2005, she urged readers of *O* magazine to give kindness as their greatest gift:

> The best gift that you can give is your goodness. It's one size fits all, it doesn't require a trip to the mall or sparkly paper, and you're not going to believe what you get back in return.

than Oprah's people originally envisioned. We're just trying to keep up with it."

Indeed, the collection boxes took on new life. Around the country, more than $1 million was deposited into them. As promised, Winfrey matched her viewers' donations by adding $1 million of her own money. Then, performer Garth Brooks contributed $1 million based on the sale of one of his albums, and movie director Jonathan Demme contributed $212,000. People watching the show wrote checks amounting to $336,000. The total earned from the piggy bank project was more than $3.5 million, and the contributions enabled the Boys and Girls Clubs of America to present several $25,000 scholarships for two years.

In 1999, a young man named Craig Kielburger, who ran a charity called Kids Can Free the Children, appeared on Winfrey's show. Kielburger talked about the projects that his organization pursued and how he wanted to educate children around the world and help them experience freedom. Kielburger had been traveling to countries like India and the Philippines to fight for children's freedom since he was 12 years old. He met children as young as five years old who were paid almost nothing to work in terrible conditions. After she and Kielburger talked more about his program, Winfrey committed the Angel Network to help build schools in many countries.

Kids Can Free the Children and Oprah's Angel Network started working together and built dozens of schools to educate thousands of children around the world. When hundreds of children showed up at a school built in Sierra Leone, not enough teachers were available to teach them. Winfrey promised that the Angel Network would also pay salaries so additional teachers could be hired. In Ecuador, Winfrey made sure that school was open for young girls who previously were never educated. "Girls often don't receive a chance to receive an education, to read or write, to learn to speak Spanish. Here in Ecuador, you can find girls 14, 15 years old who are getting married and getting pregnant," Kielburger told Winfrey's audience. "They can't own their own land, start their own business, own their own crops or cattle."

Oprah's Angel Network also seemed to have ripple effects that encouraged businesses to make donations. In St. Louis, Missouri, a home for children exposed to drugs, known as Faith House, was awarded $100,000 by the Angel Network. In the press coverage regarding the Angel Network award, the founder of Faith House spoke about a new vision that she had: a Dream House for teenagers with HIV or AIDS. Not long after, the local Anheuser-Busch Foundation wrote a check for $200,000. With that, and some other funding, a whole new project was completed. Indeed, Oprah's Angel Network was beginning to have an impact around the world.

7

The Business of
Oprah Winfrey

Oprah Winfrey was in the office of her company, Harpo Inc., in downtown Chicago with her two cocker spaniels, Sophie and Solomon, sitting at her feet. She was telling a reporter that she has never really felt like a businesswoman despite having earned more than $1 billion through her savvy business dealings.

She had become the richest black woman in the world, and millions of fans tuned into her show each day. *The Oprah Winfrey Show* had ranked first among talk shows for 20 years, and Winfrey had affected the publishing industry, the magazine industry, the film industry, and the online industry. Winfrey's businesses, by 2005, were reported to be earning an estimated $275 million each year.

Winfrey, though, was always humble. "I don't think of myself as a businesswoman," she told a reporter from *Fortune* magazine during a four-hour interview in 2002. Winfrey claimed that she did not know much about business, certainly not as much as she knew about being the host of a successful talk show. Through the years, many large corporations have invited Winfrey to sit on their boards of directors. She turned down Ralph Lauren. She turned down AT&T. She turned down Intel. The reason: She says she doesn't know much about business.

A NEW VENTURE

Winfrey's talk show made more than $300 million during 2001, and it appealed to people of both genders, as well as all races and religions. Her show was so popular that in 2000 her Harpo Entertainment Group teamed with Hearst Magazines to start *O, The Oprah Magazine*. Winfrey had appeared on a lot of magazine covers, and publishers were quite aware that she had millions of fans, partly because they sold a lot of copies whenever Winfrey's picture was on a magazine cover. Such was the case when Winfrey appeared on the cover of *Good Housekeeping* in December 1998, and 1.4 million people who were not subscribers bought the issue at a newsstand, a bookstore, or a grocery store.

"Oprah mentioned that several people had been telling her she should start a magazine," said Ellen Levine, former editor in chief of *Good Housekeeping*, when she talked to a writer from *Folio* magazine. Soon after that, Levine and another Hearst official flew to Chicago to meet with Winfrey. "Just taking a look at the success of Oprah Winfrey led us to understand the impact she can have on print," Levine said. "Her viewers are also readers—just look at the bestseller list." Winfrey's best friend, Gayle King, was named editor-at-large of the magazine and acted as a liaison between Winfrey and the staff. Winfrey, as the magazine's editorial director, approved any articles put into the magazine. In addition, it was agreed that her photo would appear on every magazine cover.

Creating a magazine may have been the next logical step for Winfrey. By 1999, her Web site, www.Oprah.com, had 7 million

Oprah Winfrey spoke about her new magazine during a press breakfast in April 2000. Behind her is the cover of the premiere issue of *O, The Oprah Magazine*. Winfrey appears on the cover of every issue.

hits each month and drew at least 2,000 e-mails from fans each day. It was apparent that Winfrey's television fans wanted to learn more. One reason Winfrey started the magazine was because she thought women weren't getting information that would help them lead better lives. She and Hearst officials agreed that women needed a guide to personal growth. In the first issue of *O*, one article encouraged women to create their own traditions for Sundays. Winfrey had always tried to keep Sundays for herself, to use as a day to regenerate her enthusiasm. Winfrey also asked some of her regular television guests, like Dr. Phil McGraw and financial expert Suze Orman, to write columns for the magazine. Winfrey had never worked on a magazine and, in the beginning, the experience was challenging. She was learning to be an editor, in addition to continuing her talk show. When *O* magazine hit the newsstands, it was considered the most successful startup in the industry. In its first full year of production, *O* magazine earned more than $140 million. And, *O* magazine proved that Winfrey was well-liked by everyone, not just people on a tight budget. Research showed that *O* readers liked Lexuses, wore Donna Karan clothing, and carried Coach bags. Everyone, it seemed, liked Winfrey—whether they were rich, poor, middle class, or new immigrants in America. Within a few years, Winfrey was also producing *O at Home*, a spin-off publication that dealt primarily with home décor.

A PARTNER IN A NETWORK

The magazine was just another of Winfrey's forays into the media industry. Winfrey was also a co-founder of the Oxygen Network, a cable television network that focused primarily on programming for women. Winfrey had previously considered starting a cable network that she would have called the Oprah Winfrey Network, or OWN, but Oxygen was the idea of a woman named Geraldine Laybourne, who had once been the president of Nickelodeon. Oxygen.com, a Web site where viewers could learn more about topics covered on the network's programs, was also part of Oxygen Media. It didn't take long to persuade Winfrey to contribute $20 million to the project and to give Oxygen some of the rights to reruns of *The Oprah Winfrey Show.*

The Oxygen Network, though, wasn't the first television network to focus mainly on women. The Lifetime channel had been in operation since 1984. The Oxygen Network struggled in its early days, and by 2002 Winfrey committed to add more of her own programming by filming the 30 minutes after each of her shows. She called the program *Oprah After the Show.* For the next several years, *Oprah After the Show* became an important program on Oxygen. Meanwhile, business at Harpo was going quite well even with Winfrey being involved in many more ventures beyond her talk show and movie company. Harpo Inc., in fact, has several divisions, including Harpo Video, which produces videos; Harpo Productions Inc., which produces the talk show; Harpo Print; and Harpo Films, which produces movies and television films.

It appeared as if Winfrey's mind never stopped working. In 2002, the day after actress Halle Berry became the first black woman to win the best actress Oscar for *Monster's Ball,* Winfrey gave Berry a call. Winfrey had decided that Berry was the right person to star in a movie Harpo was producing called *Their Eyes Were Watching God,* based on the 1937 novel of the same name by Zora Neale Hurston. "The thing is, Halle and I are friends," Winfrey once told television critics from around the country during a gathering in Los Angeles. "I really hate imposing on friends. I hate asking anybody to do anything for me, except I really, really wanted this really badly, and I only wanted her. So I thought, 'I'm going to give it a shot.'"

In fact, this wasn't the first time Winfrey had mentioned the book to Berry. In the early 1990s, Winfrey had given Berry the book after she had appeared on Winfrey's show. Berry, however, had already read the novel—during her high school years near Cleveland, Ohio. She loved the book as much as Winfrey did. In fact, Berry tried to persuade Winfrey to produce *Their Eyes Were Watching God* as a feature film, but Winfrey believed that more people would see the story if it were on television. In March 2005, Harpo released the television movie—a story that focused on how black women coped with societal pressures in the 1920s. As though to demonstrate Winfrey's wide-reaching impact, the classic book *Their Eyes Were Watching God* shot to fourth place on *Publishers Weekly's* trade paperback list immediately after the television movie had aired.

It seemed by now that nearly everything Winfrey touched turned to gold. Oprah's Book Club, in fact, had become so successful that its popularity led to its demise. "It has become harder and harder to find books on a monthly basis that I feel absolutely compelled to share," Winfrey said in April 2002 when she announced that she was canceling the regular feature on her show. Yet, Winfrey considered her book club one of her greatest achievements—she had encouraged people who had not read since high school to pick up a book and become engrossed in its meaning. In fact, several months later Winfrey reintroduced the book club but, this time, she was adamant that she would focus only on classic novels. In early 2005, a group of popular authors, including Amy Tan and Jane Smiley, wrote Winfrey a note respectfully requesting that she reconsider her position. At the time, Winfrey had made up her mind that she didn't want to get involved again with authors and publishers desperately seeking her attention. By September, though, she began to include contemporary authors once again.

A VISIT FROM MANDELA

Personally, Winfrey had grown very much. Through her years of success on her talk show, she asked questions of and had the opportunity to speak with some of the most revered people in the world. Among her heroes is Nelson Mandela, the former president of South Africa. "Today, a legend comes to life as we welcome one of the world's great heroes: Nelson Mandela," Winfrey told viewers on November 27, 2000.

One of Winfrey's heroes is Nelson Mandela, the anti-apartheid activist and former president of South Africa. Here, she and Mandela were attending the Nelson Mandela Foundation Gala Dinner in Cape Town, South Africa, in November 2003.

Mandela was one of the first activists to oppose apartheid—that is, government-imposed racial segregation—in South Africa. Blacks were prohibited by whites from voting or freely moving around their country, and stringent segregation was

Nelson Mandela

Nelson Rolihlahla Mandela was an activist who fought apartheid—a rigid system of segregation—in South Africa. Born Rolihlahla Dalibhunga Mandela on July 18, 1918, in Transkei, South Africa, he was the son of Henry Mandela and Nosekeni Fanny of the Thembu Tribe. The younger Mandela attended the University College of Fort Hare and the University of Witwatersrand, eventually becoming a lawyer. He became a member of the African National Congress (ANC) in 1942 and became an outspoken opponent to the apartheid policies of the country's ruling National Party.

In 1961, Mandela was found not guilty of treason, a charge he had fought for several years. But a year later he was sentenced to five years in prison for assisting the ANC. In 1964, Mandela and several other ANC leaders were sentenced to life in prison for plotting to overthrow the government by using violence.

While in prison, Mandela's legend grew to make him a national hero. His wife, Winnie, carried on his fight to free the country from apartheid. He became the most significant black leader in South Africa. After he was released from prison in 1990, Mandela was elected president of the ANC in 1991. The ANC and the National Party began to discuss a new multiracial democracy for South Africa. In December 1993, Mandela and Frederik Willem de Klerk, leader of South Africa's National Party, were co-recipients of the Nobel Peace Prize for their work in bringing peace to South Africa. In April 1994, for the first time in South African history, all races were permitted to vote in elections. Mandela was elected president, and the ANC won the majority of seats in the National Assembly.

imposed. In the 1950s, Mandela became a lawyer and a partner in South Africa's first black-owned law office. His protest against apartheid eventually caused him to be charged with acts of sabotage. Although he could have received the death penalty, Mandela was instead sentenced to life in prison in 1964. "Nelson Mandela's life story has become almost mythical, a testament to the power of the human spirit and one man's ability to change the world by standing up for what he believes in," Winfrey told her audience. "He is a universal hero, one of the most extraordinary people of all times, a man whose warmth, courage and unshakable commitment to freedom has inspired millions of all ages and races all around the world."

After 26 years in prison, Mandela was set free in 1990. He was a changed man who demonstrated to the world the humility, forgiveness, and love that has made him a global hero. Once he was released from prison, Mandela continued his work as an activist against apartheid. He urged the people of South Africa to work together, to talk to each other, to achieve peace and equality.

When he visited the talk show, Winfrey wanted to know how he had changed during his prison years and how he could be so forgiving to people after 26 years in captivity. "Well, I hated oppression, and when I think about the past, the type of things they did, I feel angry…," Mandela said. "You must try to use that period for the purpose of transforming your country into what you desire it to be—to a democratic, non-racial, non-sexist country."

Winfrey asked Mandela how a person could become a peacemaker inside himself. "The first thing is to be honest with yourself," Mandela said. "You can never have an impact on society if you have not changed yourself." Then, he continued, "But humility is one of the most important qualities which you must have. … Then people will embrace you. They will listen to you." Mandela is one of the people Winfrey most admires in the world. She seems to have taken his lessons to heart. In the years to come, Winfrey would concentrate even more on helping others who were less fortunate than herself.

A RENEWED FOCUS

Yet, it all wouldn't come so easily. Winfrey began giving interviews to *Fortune* magazine writer Patricia Sellers in the weeks just before September 11, 2001. Although Winfrey seemed to know what she wanted from life when she talked publicly and during her television show, she told the magazine writer, "Every time I talk to you, I feel like I'm in therapy." Later, she

IN HER OWN WORDS...

When Oprah Winfrey met young Mattie Stepanek in 2001, he was suffering from a rare form of muscular dystrophy. When Winfrey asked the youngster what he wanted for Christmas, Mattie responded, "If it's not too much trouble, pray for me." In 2004, when he was 13 years old, Mattie died. Winfrey eulogized him on her program:

When you lose a loved one, you gain an angel. That is how all those who knew this brave, ebullient and wise boy will remember him.

said that she was feeling a bit anxious, trying to figure out what to do next with her television show.

Then, September 11 occurred. On that date, terrorists crashed two planes into the World Trade Center in New York City. A third hijacked plane struck the Pentagon, and a fourth crashed in a Pennsylvania field. Thousands of people were killed. Winfrey was watching Diane Sawyer on television while her make-up was being done for the two shows to be taped that day. Gayle King called her with the latest news in New York. "I couldn't believe my eyes," said Winfrey, once she began watching the events of the day.

"The heartbreak is almost more than we can bear," Winfrey told viewers as she opened her show only two days after September 11. "We feel devastated, confused, deeply sad." On her show that day Winfrey talked to several friends and relatives who were frantically waiting for word of the life, or death, of a loved one. But none of the people could really appear in person on the show—all of them were on remote feeds because no airplanes were allowed to fly at the time. Even Dr. Phil appeared on the show via video from Texas, where he lived, to advise those watching to give themselves time to heal.

A week after the terrorist attacks of September 11, 2001, Oprah Winfrey had First Lady Laura Bush on the show to discuss terrorism and children. Following 9/11, Winfrey's shows included topics like the Muslim religion, war, and priorities in life.

Within days, First Lady Laura Bush called Winfrey and appeared on her show to talk about children and terrorism. Winfrey followed with many shows that examined the Muslim religion, war, and how people should refocus their lives. In the aftermath of the terrorist attacks, Oprah Winfrey somehow figured out what she was supposed to do next.

8

Focusing on Others

On January 28, 2004, Oprah Winfrey decided to throw herself a fiftieth birthday party, inviting 70 close friends and relatives to Chicago's Metropolitan Club high up in the Sears Tower. Her father, Vernon Winfrey, was there, and so were her friends Gayle King, Coretta Scott King, and many others. Jazz musician Ramsey Lewis serenaded Winfrey with a special version of "Happy Birthday," and Stedman Graham made a toast to Winfrey, talking about the incredible person she was. He thanked her for the encouragement and freedom that she had given him to pursue his own dreams. The evening ended with Winfrey talking about the expanse of her life and the unbelievable things that had happened in her first 50 years.

Indeed, Winfrey's life had followed an incredible path. From being a poor child in Mississippi who only wore shoes when it was time to go to church, to the wealthy, sophisticated, and influential person she was on that day, Oprah Winfrey had led a life that was nearly unbelievable. Any of her accomplishments would fulfill most people's dreams. Winfrey was the most successful talk show host in the country, and she had many other successes in the businesses she ran. In addition, she mentored her millions of viewers so they could become better contributing members of society. Winfrey started a thriving charity with the Angel Network, and she pointed her viewers toward thousands of causes that needed their help. Winfrey had succeeded in making a trip to South Africa in 2002 for her ChristmasKindness tour during which she distributed toys and clothing to thousands of children. Even though Winfrey had never become a mother, she certainly knew what children needed most—to feel loved.

In addition, Winfrey always took time out to honor the most important people in her life, like Nelson Mandela, poet Maya Angelou, and many others. When Winfrey walked onto the stage of her show the day after her birthday celebration, still more festivities were in the air. Thousands of roses—all in Winfrey's favorite pink shades—bedecked the studio as the audience waited to celebrate with the star of the hour. Chandeliers hung over the stage. Gayle King was the co-host of this birthday bash with another friend, actor John Travolta. Even the macho Travolta became emotional when he thanked Winfrey for changing the lives of millions of people. He remembered Winfrey's 2002 visit to Africa and her extravagant efforts to end famine, to fight AIDS, and to educate African children. Then, singer Tina Turner whipped the crowd into a frenzy by serenading Winfrey with her song, "Simply the Best." Stevie Wonder showed up to sing, too. Videotaped thank-yous and best wishes from several people around the world were played, including a group of African girls who gave thanks to Mama Oprah. *Tonight Show* host Jay Leno wheeled out a 400-pound banana-flavored birthday cake decorated with sugar roses and edible gold-trimmed, handpainted portraits of Winfrey.

DID YOU KNOW?

Oprah Winfrey's growing interest in her African roots led her to have her DNA tested in 2005. She wanted to learn about her African tribal ancestry. On a visit to South Africa, she reported to a group in Johannesburg that her heritage was Zulu. Her announcement caused debate in South Africa, and her claim was rebuffed by some prominent Zulus.

Prince Mangosuthu Buthelezi, leader of the country's Zulus, said that Winfrey must be mistaken—there were no records of Zulus who had been taken to America as slaves. People around the world continued to debate whether Winfrey's DNA testing could be accurate.

The search into the past for Winfrey and eight other notable people was documented in *African American Lives*, a show aired on PBS in early 2006. The people who tested the DNA for the program concluded that Winfrey was probably descended from the Kpelle people, who lived in present-day Liberia.

A parade of congratulations continued with taped tributes from Steven Spielberg, Tom Cruise, Julia Roberts, Halle Berry—who was dressed in a leather Catwoman outfit, a costume from the movie she was working on—and others. Winfrey's handpicked audience of 300 special guests went home with T-shirts, pajamas, tote bags, and journals. Before leaving the studio, they enjoyed a special birthday lunch prepared by famous chef Wolfgang Puck and were entertained by pop star Josh Groban and a band from South Africa.

Winfrey's birthday festivities did not stop there, either. On Friday afternoon, January 30, she flew to Los Angeles where she met a group of women—called her 50 most fabulous women—at the Hotel Bel-Air for lunch. Then, she threw a dinner party at her California ranch. Another huge bash was planned for the following day when she entertained the people who couldn't make it to Chicago—Halle Berry, Tom Cruise,

Julia Roberts, and many more, including old friend Maria Shriver and her husband, Arnold Schwarzenegger, who by then was the governor of California.

Indeed, Winfrey had come a long way from the years as a child whose mother left her to live with her grandmother while young Oprah wondered if anybody really cared about her. Winfrey had plenty of friends, millions of adoring fans, and more money than she could have ever imagined. She still lived in her penthouse in Chicago, but she also had a house in Maui and a huge estate in California. Years earlier, she had sold her Indiana farm, but she had also owned houses in Colorado. When Winfrey toured the country and gave "Live Your Best Life" seminars, thousands of women showed up for the day-long pep talk, which cost $185. In the meantime, she jetted around the world for various functions and charities, including a 2003 trip to Johannesburg, South Africa, to attend Nelson Mandela's eighty-fifth birthday celebration.

GIFTS FOR HER FANS

Although the famed talk show host focused on a full range of international topics, *The Oprah Winfrey Show* was still popular among its fans for doing wild and crazy stunts. For example, to open her nineteenth season in 2004, Winfrey handed out the keys to 276 Pontiac vehicles to an audience that included many people who desperately needed new cars. Each person in Winfrey's audience received a small gift box and was told to open it to see if it contained the key to a car. Within seconds, the audience was in bedlam when all those attending the show discovered keys in their boxes. "You get a car. You get a car. You get a car. You get a car," Winfrey said as she walked around the stage pointing to different people. The audience members—mainly women—screamed and hugged one another. "Your cars are waiting right outside," Winfrey said, as the parking lot full of Pontiacs was shown on a big screen on the stage. More screaming filled the air.

That day the ratings for Winfrey's show shot higher than they had been in years, and the traffic on Oprah.com increased by 800 percent. News of Winfrey's gimmick traveled around the world—with articles and broadcasters talking about it in all of the 121 countries that carried the show. Although Pontiac donated the cars to Winfrey's audience, a second round of news articles appeared when the new car owners realized that they would have to pay federal taxes—amounting to $7,000—on each of the vehicles.

Despite the fun, Winfrey still dealt with important issues, like the crisis in South Africa, child abuse, and other such topics. Winfrey also occasionally entertained her audience with stars. One of the most talked-about shows occurred in May 2005 when Tom Cruise visited and jumped on her sofa in front of the cameras. "I'm in love!" he exclaimed about actress Katie Homes. Many months later, Winfrey said, "I was thinking, 'What has happened to the boy.'"

Over the years of hosting her show, acting in movies, and appearing on the cover of her magazine, Winfrey has become as much of a celebrity as most of those she interviews. She has received praise from many actors and actresses. Those who appeared on her show sometimes were nearly awestruck, while others cried when they finally met her. And Winfrey continued to collect various awards. In 2004, she and the editor in chief of O magazine, Amy Gross, received Adweek magazine's top honor as Editors of the Year. Winfrey continued to be very involved in every issue of the magazine, even though its offices were based in New York. She talked with Gross at least once a week, and they exchanged e-mails even more frequently. Winfrey read each magazine page—e-mailed or shipped overnight to her—before it was printed. In all, she spent at least three hours a day on each issue of O.

Meanwhile, Winfrey's show continued to be popular with fans trying hard to get tickets. Winfrey taped 145 shows a year, and only 300 people could sit in the audience each time.

Still, even with 43,500 people able to watch a show in one year, many more people never got through the doors. One of the most amazing annual shows is called "Oprah's Favorite Things." During one episode, an audience member even fainted when she saw the many free items that Winfrey gave her and the others attending the program.

Teachers from across the United States were flown to Chicago for the show on November 22, 2004. "The entire audience is filled with teachers from all over, every state including Hawaii," Winfrey said during the show's introductions. "And why are they here? Because I have said this at least a thousand times: I love teachers!" In fact, she had often said that if she were not a talk show host, she would be a teacher. During the show, Winfrey proceeded to give each teacher a Burberry jacket and scarf set, a flat screen television, lipstick, a washer and a dryer, bubble bath, a leather duffle bag, a spa getaway in Arizona, a watch, more clothing, an automobile satellite system, a laptop computer, and more. Before the show, she had taped a visit to Office Max, an office supply store. Winfrey nearly wept when she came across the big boxes of 64 crayons—they reminded her of her eighth Christmas when her father and stepmother gave her crayons and paper as a gift. Office Max donated $500 gift certificates to each teacher in her audience. "My Christmas prayer is that love will spread throughout every heart, that love will rule and reign," Winfrey told her audience as she closed the show.

RECOGNIZED FOR HER PHILANTHROPY

Meanwhile, Winfrey continued to be honored for her work. Instead of collecting awards aimed just at her television show, however, Winfrey began accumulating worldwide praise for her philanthropy and goodwill. In 2002, Winfrey received the first Bob Hope Humanitarian Award at the Primetime Emmy Awards. "Like Bob Hope, Oprah has become an icon of her generation whom we love to invite into our homes over and over," announced Bryce Zabel, chairman of the Academy of Television Arts and Sciences. "Oprah as an entertainer provokes thought, discussion, debate and empowers women, all in a graceful, direct, and honest style that we have all come to know and respect."

A few years later, Winfrey was presented the 2004 Global Humanitarian Action Award by the United Nations Association of the United States of America, a nonprofit group that supports the work of the United Nations. She was praised during the ceremony by U.S. Senator Hillary Rodham Clinton and

Oprah Winfrey accepts the Bob Hope Humanitarian Award during the Primetime Emmy Awards in 2002. Behind her is actor Tom Hanks, who presented the award. "Like Bob Hope, Oprah has become an icon of her generation whom we love to invite into our homes over and over," said Bryce Zabel, chairman of the Academy of Television Arts and Sciences.

IN HER OWN WORDS...

Oprah Winfrey received the Bob Hope Humanitarian Award, the first time it was ever presented, at the Primetime Emmy Awards on September 22, 2002. She said the following during her acceptance speech:

> The greatest pain in life is to be invisible. What I've learned is that we all just want to be heard. And I thank all the people who continue to let me hear your stories, and by sharing your stories, you let other people see themselves and for a moment, glimpse the power to change and the power to triumph.

actor Michael Douglas. United Nations Secretary-General Kofi Annan said at the presentation:

> Oprah, your ability to connect with others has touched the hearts and lives of millions of viewers. I can tell you, I sometimes feel envious in my dealings with world leaders, and I wish I had your communication skills. And you have used your skills and your empathy to go far beyond the world of television entertainment. Through your passionate commitment to education, health, and the cause of women's empowerment and the fight against HIV/AIDS worldwide, you have given many people around the world the gift of hope—a hope for a better life.

In November 2005, Winfrey received the National Freedom Award from the National Civil Rights Museum for her work with children in Africa and for helping to create a database of convicted child abusers. Winfrey was inducted into the NAACP Hall of Fame in 2005, and her philanthropic work and her heartfelt empathy for people around the world has some of her fans even talking about a Nobel Peace Prize in the future. Indeed, Winfrey seemed to collect a different award every week. Certainly, after all of her struggles with weight and self-image, one of the awards that probably amazed Winfrey the most was to be listed among the top 10 best-dressed women on *Vanity Fair*'s International Best Dressed List in 2004 and 2005.

Still, Winfrey stayed focused on honoring other people. In May 2005, Winfrey held a weekend bash to honor women who are her heroes. Among them were 25 black women who had made large contributions in arts, entertainment, and civil rights—women who had been "a bridge to now," in Winfrey's words. The women received hand-embroidered invitations, and no one knew who else would be attending. Tina Turner, Maya Angelou, Coretta Scott King, Gladys Knight, Diana Ross, and several others gathered for a celebration that began with a Friday luncheon at Winfrey's California estate. Each woman had her own personal waiter and was served flower pots created from chocolate cake and icing for dessert. The guests—who numbered beyond 60, including young black women like Halle Berry and Janet Jackson—received red alligator gift boxes containing engraved silver boxes and diamond earrings. The Legends Weekend celebration continued with a star-studded ball on Saturday evening at a nearby resort, where her guests ate tuna flown in from Japan while a 26-piece orchestra entertained them. "Oprah told me that this has been one of the most extraordinary events of her life," Gayle King told a writer for *USA Today* when the weekend was over. "We never could have anticipated such a love fest between the generations."

Winfrey's respect and admiration for the successful black women who came before her, as well as her own black heritage, continued to be a driving force in her work. She joined her friend Quincy Jones and others in a drive to raise funds for a government-sponsored National Museum of African-American History and Culture, which would be part of the Smithsonian Institution in Washington, D.C. The museum was expected to include videotaped oral histories of black people, photographs of lynchings in the Southern United States, chains from slave ships that came from Africa, and other such artifacts.

In May 2005, Oprah Winfrey held her Legends Weekend celebration to honor 25 pioneering African-American women who had made contributions to civil rights, the arts, and entertainment. Here, she arrives at the Legends Ball, which was part of the weekend bash.

Meanwhile, Winfrey's work in South Africa and around the world continued to move forward. Since it began in 1997, Oprah's Angel Network had raised more than $27 million. The network had helped purchase school uniforms and supplies for children in South Africa, and it supported organizations that help women and children in different parts of the world. In 2005, nine students from Morehouse College in Atlanta kicked off the Oprah South African Leadership Project, which was financed by a $1 million grant from Winfrey. Students who participated in the program studied ethical leadership training and community service, in Atlanta and in South Africa. Oprah's Angel Network also built schools in 11 countries—China, Ecuador, Ghana, Guatemala, Haiti, India, Mexico, Nicaragua, Kenya, Sierra Leone, and Tanzania.

In addition, Oprah's Angel Network began to provide books for children in certain regions of the world based on

Emmy Awards

In 2005, Oprah Winfrey earned a special award—she was presented with an International Emmy Founders Award for her international broadcasting career and her philanthropic endeavors. The latest award just tops off Winfrey's long history of receiving Emmy Awards. In fact, she is among only 100 people who have been inducted to the Emmy Hall of Fame.

What is an Emmy Award? Emmy Awards recognize excellence within the television industry. The Academy of Television Arts and Sciences honors prime-time programming, while the National Academy of Television Arts and Sciences recognizes achievement in daytime, sports, news, and documentary programs. The mission of the academies is to promote creativity, diversity, innovation, and excellence by recognizing education and leadership in telecommunications arts and sciences.

The International Award that Winfrey received in 2005 was given by the International Academy of Television Arts and Sciences, which was started in 1969 and represents more than 500 broadcasters across the world. In total, Winfrey and *The Oprah Winfrey Show* have received more than 40 Daytime Emmy Awards, including 7 awards for outstanding talk show host, 9 for outstanding talk show, and more than 20 in the creative arts. Winfrey received another Emmy for her work as supervising producer of the ABC After-school Special *Shades of a Single Protein*.

where an Oprah's Book Club selection was set. For example, a Pearl S. Buck book called *The Good Earth,* which is set in China, was purchased in mass quantity and distributed in Beijing to children who could not afford to buy books. In 2000, the network started the Use Your Life Award, which has given grants totaling more than $6 million to individuals who are making a difference through their charitable groups. The money has helped small- to mid-size groups expand their programs.

Even though it may appear that her business interests are quite broad—with her show, her magazine, and her film production company—Winfrey expanded her empire even more. In 2005, she agreed to invest in a Broadway musical version of *The Color Purple.* By being an investor and producer of the musical, Winfrey hoped to expose her viewers to a Broadway show, just as she has opened the door for many viewers to begin reading books.

Meanwhile, Oprah's Book Club continued to evolve after it was revived in 2003 with the aim of choosing only classical novels. For the first time since resuming the club, Winfrey selected a book by a contemporary author, the memoir *A Million Little Pieces* by James Frey. "Education and transformation through reading are part of her mission," an editor for *Publishers Weekly* told writer Caitlin Kelley. "The intimacy of the relationship between the writer and the reader is paralleled by the intimacy Oprah has with her viewers."

A bit of controversy dogged Oprah's Book Club in early 2006, though, after it was discovered that Frey had fabricated parts of *A Million Little Pieces.* Winfrey at first defended the book when Frey appeared on CNN's *Larry King Show.* On her own show a few weeks later, though, she confronted Frey about his lies and criticized Frey's publisher for not checking the accuracy of his book. Some in the publishing field say that Winfrey's clout will cause the industry to change the way it fact-checks nonfiction books.

With all of her popularity, it seems as if Winfrey cannot make a move without the media and all of her fans taking interest. Tabloid newspapers were abuzz when she showed up at the NAACP Image Awards in 2005 without Stedman Graham, but Winfrey and Graham continued to keep the details of their relationship very private. Then, a few months later, news that Winfrey had been closed out of the Hermes store in Paris one afternoon caused a stir. The store said that it was closed to stage a public relations event inside when Winfrey showed up to buy a watch for a friend and was promptly asked to leave. It was apparent, though, through comments from Winfrey's spokesperson, that the talk show host felt an element of racial discrimination had been involved. Certainly, Winfrey's life is rarely dull. Newspaper and magazine articles about her abound. There is continuous talk about how long she would keep her show on television, whether she can keep her topics fresh, and whether her viewers will grow tired of her. Yet, through it all, Winfrey continued to provide an invigorating mix of intriguing, startling, and soothing information to her millions of fans.

THE LEGACY

Winfrey had tears in her eyes as one of her heroes, Sidney Poitier, read a poem to her on the stage in front of the studio audience. It was November 2005, and Winfrey had just finished telling her audience that Poitier had been an inspiration when she, at 10 years old, watched him win an Academy Award. At the time, Poitier was the lone black star among many white men. "I thought it unfair," Poitier had once told Winfrey when he appeared on her show years earlier. But on this special celebration of the twentieth anniversary of *The Oprah Winfrey Show*, Poitier was proud to be the single celebrity joining Winfrey onstage to honor her genius among all people, black and white.

"Let's face it, there was nobody that looked like me," said Winfrey, as she introduced her show that day. It's true: When

Winfrey arrived in Chicago and when her show became syndicated two years later—no one on television looked like her. She was a woman, she was black, she was overweight, and she wore her hair in an Afro. Today, it's not unusual for Winfrey to refer to herself as "a former colored girl" because her lifetime has spanned a period of more than 50 years in which the United States has become more diverse and people of all colors are treated with more respect. Winfrey is among the public personas who have helped change the way black Americans are perceived and the way they perceive themselves. And, she has given hope to all people—no matter their color or class—that they can use their abilities to flourish as human beings. In her life, she has seemingly been through it all. Winfrey has been victorious over poverty, child abuse, and discrimination, and all along she has been open and honest about her feelings in front of millions of television viewers.

Winfrey has lived the American Dream. Her rise to fame and fortune, as well as the stories of the people who have appeared on her television show, has been the impetus for many women and men to improve their lives. Winfrey has been the role model for many people of different races to live their lives to the fullest, to strive for the best, and to share with others the riches that their lives bring to them. Her generosity, perhaps, is the trait that may outlive her television show, her magazine, and other parts of her businesses. Oprah's Angel Network continues to give to a variety of causes, including a 2005 donation of $1 million to the Free the Children Fund, Habitat for Humanity, and a group called Mercy Corps to rebuild schools, provide supplies and health care, and produce clean water in an area of Sri Lanka that was devastated by the tsunami of December 2004.

Meanwhile, Winfrey's legendary trip to South Africa in 2002 was startling among the work of other celebrities and billionaires across the world. She accomplished an amazing feat when, as an important talk show host, she traveled to a poverty-stricken country to spend her days with children who had been orphaned because of AIDS, whose lives are lived in lonely huts, and who sleep on dirt floors. Winfrey has reached far beyond the television personality that she spent years creating. She has become one of the world's most important philanthropists—not only through what she can afford to donate herself, but through her ability to motivate others to contribute to many causes.

When Hurricane Katrina hit New Orleans and the Gulf Coast in September 2005, she quickly took *The Oprah Winfrey Show* to the region to expose the catastrophe in her own style. Winfrey called on friends Faith Hill, Jamie Foxx, and others to talk about the recovery. She met with New Orleans Mayor Ray Nagin and went inside the Superdome to investigate the violence and rapes that were reported to have occurred there. Then, Winfrey topped it all off by introducing the Angel Network's Hurricane Katrina relief fund to help rebuild houses and to purchase household items for hurricane victims. Oprah's Katrina Home Registry at www.Oprah.com encouraged fans to contribute funding for items ranging from a park bench for $10 to a full kitchen for $1,555 to a complete house for $50,000. In addition, Oprah.com listed other major agencies and organizations—like the American Red Cross, the Salvation Army, the United Way, America's Second Harvest, and others—to help make it easier for her fans to make contributions. Oprah.com directed people to organizations that would help them find children and adults missing in the aftermath of the storm. Winfrey even made pet rescue an important part of the discussion and encouraged her viewers to contribute to the American Society for the Prevention of Cruelty to Animals (ASPCA), the Humane Society of the United States, and other animal-friendly organizations.

Not only does Winfrey use her financial clout to make changes in society, she also encourages her huge network of television fans to participate in these changes. The programming that she developed for her 2005 television season spoke loudly to the changes that Winfrey hoped to make. Following her on-location shows on Hurricane Katrina, Winfrey launched into another emotional topic. She offered $100,000 to any of her viewers who helped catch noted child abusers and molesters. "I plan to work with law enforcement officials, and if they tell me that one of you turned in one of these fugitives that we're exposing today, and that information leads to the capture and arrest of one of these men, I will personally give a $100,000 reward," Winfrey announced on her show. Within 48 hours, two men on the list were caught with help from her viewers—one of the wanted men was in Fargo, North Dakota, and the other was in Belize City, Belize. Winfrey's wide span of fans around the world has developed into a formidable force for those trying to escape the law. But, more than that, Winfrey's fans have become part of a profound phenomena created by one woman who liked to talk and built on those skills to create a media empire.

The little girl who was once referred to as "The Preacher" by her schoolmates has become much more than that. As the wealthiest black woman in the world, Oprah Winfrey has earned respect and admiration from people of all races and religions. Only the talk show host herself knows what her future will bring. But fans can be sure that Winfrey's power and prestige, her honor and her honesty, have limitless boundaries. Certainly, the first 50 years of Oprah Winfrey's life are only the beginning of the rest of her story.

Oprah Winfrey in Film and Television

AS AN ACTRESS

The Color Purple (1985) Sofia

Native Son (1986) Mrs. Thomas

The Women of Brewster Place (1989) (TV) Mattie Michael

There Are No Children Here (1993) (TV) LaJoe Rivers

Before Women Had Wings (1997) (TV) Miss Zora

Beloved (1998) Sethe

AS A PRODUCER

The Oprah Winfrey Show (1986–present) (TV) supervising
producer

The Women of Brewster Place (1989) (TV) executive producer

Nine (1992) (TV) executive producer

Overexposed (1992) (TV) executive producer

Before Women Had Wings (1997) (TV) producer

The Wedding (1998) (TV) executive producer

Beloved (1998) producer

David and Lisa (1998) (TV) executive producer

Tuesdays With Morrie (1999) (TV) executive producer

Amy and Isabelle (2001) (TV) executive producer, producer

Their Eyes Were Watching God (2005) (TV) executive producer

Selected Picks from Oprah's Book Club

Oprah Winfrey began her book club in 1996 as a segment on her talk show. She suspended the club in 2002, but restored it a year later, with a new focus on classic works of literature. In the fall of 2005, Winfrey again began to select contemporary books. Here is a look at some of Winfrey's selections over the years:

The Deep End of the Ocean by Jacquelyn Mitchard (selected September 1996): In Mitchard's first novel, a three-year-old boy from a middle-class family is kidnapped from the lobby of a hotel, where his mother has taken him and his two siblings to attend her fifteenth high school reunion. The kidnapping tears the family apart as each member reacts in varying ways. Then, nine years later, the missing son shows up and offers to mow the family's lawn. And again, everything changes.

Song of Solomon by Toni Morrison (October 1996): Morrison's 1977 novel follows four generations of black life in the United States, seen through the protagonist Macon "Milkman" Dead III. The novel won the National Book Critics Circle Award and was cited when Morrison was awarded the 1993 Nobel Prize in literature.

Stones From the River by Ursula Hegi (February 1997): Born in 1915, the novel's protagonist, a dwarf named Trudi Montag, grows up in Germany between the two world wars. Trudi identifies with underdogs like herself. As Hitler rises to power, the book depicts the effects on ordinary people and the chances that Trudi and her father must take.

The Heart of a Woman by Maya Angelou (May 1997): Angelou's fourth volume of autobiography (the first was *I Know Why the Caged Bird Sings*) looks at her life in the late 1950s and early 1960s—a heady time for Angelou. She was starting to become a writer and was also actively involved in the civil-rights movement, meeting with the Reverend Dr. Martin Luther King, Jr., and Malcolm X. Just as important is her relationship with her teenage son, also described in the book.

A Lesson Before Dying by Ernest J. Gaines (September 1997): In 1940s Louisiana, a young black man named Jefferson is to be executed. He was an innocent bystander to a shootout that left a white shopkeeper and two black robbers dead, but Jefferson was convicted of murder nonetheless. Grant, another young black man who has a university education, returns to the town and can only get a job as a teacher in the plantation church school. Jefferson's godmother asks Grant to teach Jefferson to die like a man. The relationship between the two men transforms them both.

Breath, Eyes, Memory by Edwidge Danticat (May 1998): Danticat's 1994 coming-of-age novel is about Sophie, who grows up in Haiti in the care of an aunt. As a teenager, she leaves for New York to live with her mother. Later, she and her mother become estranged, and Sophie returns to Haiti to ease some of her confusion.

What Looks Like Crazy on an Ordinary Day by Pearl Cleage (September 1998): Ava Johnson, who has lived in Atlanta for 10 years, discovers she is HIV-positive. She decides to move to San Francisco but first will spend the summer with her recently widowed sister in their childhood home of Idlewild, Michigan. There, she becomes enmeshed in some big-city problems. With Cleage's sharp and humorous attitude, this book manages to avoid maudlin melodrama.

Jewel by Bret Lott (January 1999): This novel, which spans decades, begins in 1943 in Mississippi, where Jewel Hilburn, her husband, Leston, and their five children live. The wartime economy is booming, and the family is doing well. At 40, Jewel is pregnant again, and the child, Brenda, turns out to have Down syndrome. Jewel, who rebuffs the doctor's suggestion that the child be sent to an institution, leads her family on a journey to California and establishes a mother-daughter bond that strengthens everyone.

The Reader by Bernhard Schlink (February 1999): Written by a German judge, this novel is told in three parts by the main character,

Michael Berg. Michael is 15 years old in the first section, which takes place in 1958. The novel looks at the difficulties in comprehending the Holocaust as experienced by the generations that are growing up after it occurred.

Tara Road by Maeve Binchy (September 1999): Two women, one from Ireland and the other from the United States, trade houses without having met. The Irish woman, Ria Lynch, has been left by her husband. The American woman, Marilyn Vine, is coping with her son's death. The house swap is a way for both women to escape their problems, but they also end up discovering a great deal about themselves and each other.

River, Cross My Heart by Breena Clarke (October 1999): Clarke's debut novel is set in 1925 among the large and close-knit black community in the Georgetown section of Washington, D.C. The story centers on the drowning of 8-year-old Clara Bynum in the Potomac River and her death's effect on her family and neighbors—particularly the impact on her 12-year-old sister, Johnnie Mae, who was baby-sitting Clara when she drowned.

Gap Creek by Robert Morgan (January 2000): This novel, set at the turn of the twentieth century in the Appalachian high country, follows the life of 17-year-old Julie Harmon and her husband, Hank, in their first year of marriage. They are deeply in love, but they must endure fire, flood, swindlers, and starvation.

Daughter of Fortune by Isabel Allende (February 2000): Set in the mid-1800s, the novel tells the story of Eliza Sommers, a Chilean by birth who is adopted by an English brother and sister who live in Valparaiso, Chile. A pregnant Eliza follows her lover as he seeks his fortune in the California gold rush of 1849. Along the way she meets a Chinese doctor who saves her life and becomes her friend. What begins as a search for a lost love becomes a voyage of self-discovery.

The Poisonwood Bible by Barbara Kingsolver (June 2000): The book tells of a missionary family's life in the Congo starting in

1959. It is written with five narrative voices, corresponding to the five women in the family—the mother and four daughters. The fate of the family is intertwined with that of the Congo over three decades.

We Were the Mulvaneys by Joyce Carol Oates (January 2001): The Mulvaneys, living in rural New York, seem like the perfect family. They run a successful roofing business, and each of the four children seems to excel. Then, the daughter is raped by a classmate whose father is a friend of Mr. Mulvaney's. The rape is hushed up in town and never spoken of by the Mulvaneys. In the aftermath, the family disintegrates. More than a decade later, the Mulvaneys come together and begin to heal.

Stolen Lives: Twenty Years in a Desert Jail by Malika Oufkir (May 2001): Oufkir was the eldest daughter of General Oufkir, the king of Morocco's closest aide. At age 5, she was adopted by the king and sent to live in the palace as part of the royal court. In 1972, her father was found guilty of treason after staging a coup. Oufkir, her mother, and her five siblings were arrested, despite having no prior knowledge of the coup attempt. They were first held at an abandoned fort and then in a remote desert prison. Conditions deteriorated until they suffered solitary confinement, torture, and starvation. The deprivations they experience are in stark contrast to the luxuries Oufkir enjoyed in her early life.

A Fine Balance by Rohinton Mistry (November 2001): This novel is set in an unnamed city by the sea in India in the late 1970s during a period of government crackdowns on civil liberties. The story follows four ordinary people from varied backgrounds—a widow, a student, and two tailors escaping caste violence—as they come together and develop a bond in their efforts to survive.

Fall on Your Knees by Ann-Marie MacDonald (January 2002): This book by MacDonald, a Canadian actress and playwright, is a sprawling tale of five generations of a family from Nova

Scotia. Its focus is on four sisters and their relationships with one another and with their father. The novel is full of family history and family secrets.

East of Eden by John Steinbeck (June 2003): Steinbeck's classic 1952 novel details the interwoven lives of two families, the Trasks and the Hamiltons, in the Salinas Valley of California in the early twentieth century. The Hamiltons, immigrants from Ireland, raise nine children on unfertile land. As the children grow up, Adam Trask moves onto a fertile plot nearby, helped by the wealth of his dead father. The book examines poverty and wealth, love, and guilt and freedom. Through the characters, Steinbeck retells the fall of Adam and Eve and the rivalry of Cain and Abel.

Cry, the Beloved Country by Alan Paton (September 2003): This 1948 novel by South African author Alan Paton depicts the Reverend Stephen Kumalo, a black pastor in a village, and his search for his son Absalom in Johannesburg. Absalom has been arrested for the murder of Arthur Jarvis, a white fighter for racial justice, and is later sentenced to death. Arthur's father, James, is a neighbor of Pastor Kumalo's. James Jarvis reads his son's writings and decides to take up his work. Kumalo returns to his barren village, and help arrives when James Jarvis becomes involved in the work to improve farming conditions. The book ends on the night of Absalom's execution.

One Hundred Years of Solitude by Gabriel Garcia Márquez (January 2004): The novel spans 100 years in the life of a small Colombian town called Macondo. A theme of the book is that reality is subjective and depends on a person's perceptions. The book, first published in Spanish in 1967, is considered Garcia Márquez's masterpiece.

The Heart Is a Lonely Hunter by Carson McCullers (April 2004): This 1940 novel focuses on John Singer, who is deaf and mute, and the people he meets in a Georgia mill town in the 1930s. These people include a 14-year-old girl, Mick Kelly, whose poor family takes in boarders; Jake Blount, a volatile labor agitator who often rants about socialism; Biff Brannon, the owner of a local café; and Dr. Benedict Copeland, an older black doctor who is angered by the injustices blacks suffer.

Anna Karenina by Leo Tolstoy (May 2004): Anna Karenina is an upstanding member of St. Petersburg society until she leaves her husband for a military officer, Count Vronsky. Tragedy follows as neither is strong enough to withstand society's retaliation. Anna cannot return to her husband, whom she detests, and she cannot accept Vronsky's rejection. Contrasting this is the joyous, honest relationship of Konstantin and Kitty. Konstantin is a wealthy landowner who prefers to work his land. He unsuccessfully tries to fit into aristocratic circles when he is courting Kitty. But he only wins her over when he is true to himself. First published in 1877, *Anna Karenina* is considered Tolstoy's best book.

The Good Earth by Pearl S. Buck (September 2004): Published in 1931, Buck's novel won the Pulitzer Prize in 1932. The book tells the story of a peasant family in China as its members live through famine, flood, and prosperity—both in the country and in the city.

Night by Elie Wiesel (January 2006): This autobiographical novella is based on Wiesel's experience as a young Jew during World War II. He and his family were deported from their village in Transylvania to the German concentration camp at Auschwitz. There, he and his father were separated from his mother and sisters. Wiesel's mother and a sister were killed; his two other sisters managed to survive. Wiesel and his father were later sent to the Buchenwald concentration camp, where they remained together until his father's death only a few weeks before the camp was liberated.

1954 Oprah Winfrey is born on January 29 in Kosciusko, Mississippi

1960 Moves to Milwaukee to be with her mother and half-sister

1968 Moves to live with her father, Vernon Winfrey, and his wife, Zelma, in Nashville, Tennessee

1971 Wins the title of Miss Fire Prevention in Nashville; becomes a part-time newscaster at WVOL radio station in Nashville

1972 Wins the Miss Black Nashville beauty pageant and gets a four-year scholarship to Tennessee State University; wins the Miss Black Tennessee beauty pageant and competes in the Miss Black America pageant.

1973 Becomes a weekend news co-anchor at WTVF-TV in Nashville

1976 Becomes an evening news co-anchor at WJZ-TV in Baltimore, Maryland

1977 Is named co-host of a WJZ talk show called *People Are Talking*

1983 Is hired to host *A.M. Chicago* at WLS-TV

1985 *A.M. Chicago* becomes *The Oprah Winfrey Show*; Winfrey plays a supporting role in the film *The Color Purple*

1986 Is nominated for an Academy Award for *The Color Purple*; *The Oprah Winfrey Show* becomes nationally syndicated

1988 Founds Harpo Productions; Harpo produces *The Women of Brewster Place*; Winfrey is the youngest recipient ever of the Broadcaster of the Year Award, given by the International Radio and Television Society

1991 Testifies before the U.S. Senate Judiciary Committee to support the National Child Protection Act

1992 Becomes engaged to Stedman Graham

1993 Wins a Horatio Alger Award; President Bill Clinton signs the National Child Protection Act

1996 Starts Oprah's Book Club; wins the International Radio and Television Society Foundation's Gold Medal Award; receives the George Foster Peabody Individual Achievement Award

1997 Produces and stars in the television movie *Before Women Had Wings;* is named *Newsweek*'s Most Important Person in Books and Media; is named Television Performer of the Year by *TV Guide*

1998 Produces and stars in *Beloved,* based on Toni Morrison's novel; wins lawsuit filed by Texas cattle ranchers after her show on mad cow disease; produces the television movie *The Wedding;* receives Daytime Emmy for Lifetime Achievement and removes herself from future Emmy consideration the following year; is named one of the 100 Most Influential People of the 20th Century by *Time* magazine; becomes a co-founder of the Oxygen Network; forms Oprah's Angel Network

1999 Receives National Book Foundation's 50th Anniversary Gold Medal; produces the television movie *Tuesdays With Morrie*

2000 Launches *O, The Oprah Magazine*

2002 Receives the Bob Hope Humanitarian Award at the 54th Annual Primetime Emmy Awards; is named to the Broadcasting and Cable Hall of Fame; releases the first international edition of *O, The Oprah Magazine* in South Africa

2003 Receives the Association of American Publishers' AAP Honors Award

2004 Receives the United Nations Association of the United States of America Global Humanitarian Action Award;

receives National Association of Broadcasters Distin-
guished Service Award; is named among the 100 Most
Influential People in the World by *Time* magazine;
releases *O at Home*, a quarterly publication about
homes and decorating

2005   Is named to the NAACP Hall of Fame; receives the
National Freedom Award from the National Civil Rights
Museum; is presented the International Emmy Founders
Award; is named among the 100 Most Influential People
of the World by *Time* magazine; releases *The Oprah
Winfrey Show: 20th Anniversary DVD Collection*, with
proceeds going to Oprah's Angel Network

Adler, Bill, editor. *The Uncommon Wisdom of Oprah Winfrey: A Portrait in Her Own Words.* New York: Citadel Press, 1999.

Garson, Helen S. *Oprah Winfrey: A Biography.* Westport, CT: Greenwood Press, 2004.

Greene, Bob and Oprah Winfrey, *Make the Connection: Ten Steps to a Better Body and a Better Life.* New York: Hyperion, 1996.

Krohn, Katherine E. *Oprah Winfrey.* Minneapolis: Lerner Publications Company, 2002.

Live Your Best Life: A Treasury of Wisdom, Wit, Advice, Interviews, and Inspiration From O, The Oprah Magazine. Birmingham, AL: Oxmoor House, 2005.

Lowe, Janet. *Oprah Winfrey Speaks: Insight From the World's Most Influential Voice.* New York: John Wiley & Sons, Inc., 1998.

Mair, George. *Oprah Winfrey: The Real Story.* New York: Carol Publishing Group, 1994.

Mayer, Larry. *Oprah Winfrey: The Soul and Spirit of a Superstar.* Chicago: Triumph Books, 2000.

Rooney, Kathleen. *Reading With Oprah: The Book Club That Changed America.* Fayetteville, AR: University of Arkansas Press, 2005.

Westen, Robin. *Oprah Winfrey: "I Don't Believe in Failure."* Berkeley Heights, NJ: Enslow Publishers, 2005.

Winfrey, Oprah. *Journey to Beloved.* New York: Hyperion, 1998.

Wooten, Sara McIntosh. *Oprah Winfrey: Talk Show Legend.* Berkeley Heights, NJ: Enslow Publishers, 1999.

WEB SITES

Fem-Biography: Oprah Winfrey
www.fembio.org/women/oprah-winfrey.shtml

Oprah.com
www.oprah.com

Oprah's Angel Network
www.oprahsangelnetwork.org

Oprah Winfrey biography
www.gale.com/free_resources/bhm/bio/winfrey_o.html

Oprah Winfrey profile—Academy of Achievement
http://www.achievement.org/autodoc/page/win0pro-1

Quotations by Oprah Winfrey
www.quotationspage.com/quotes/Oprah_Winfrey

Time 100: Oprah Winfrey
http://www.time.com/time/time100/artists/profile/winfrey.html

Index

Picture Credits

page:

Sherry Beck Paprocki is a freelance journalist and has written or contributed to six books for children, including *World Leaders: Vicente Fox* (Chelsea House, 2002); *Women of Achievement: Katie Couric* (Chelsea House, 2001); and *Women Who Win: Michelle Kwan* (Chelsea House, 2001). In addition, her bylines have appeared in *Pages* magazine, *Preservation* magazine, *The Chicago Tribune*, the *Cleveland Plain Dealer*, *The Philadelphia Inquirer*, the Los Angeles Times Syndicate, and many other publications. She is a graduate of The Ohio State University School of Journalism and lives near Columbus, Ohio, where she also serves as an adjunct faculty member of Otterbein College.